All of us are on journeys. So few are on so great a journey as Dr. Haywood Robinson and Dr. Noreen Johnson, who traveled from performing abortions to being pro-life champions. *The Scalpel and the Soul* reveals the story of this couple and reflects the stories of so many other medical professionals who, once confronted with the real truth about abortion, can no longer stay where they are but must journey toward the truth about life. You won't regret taking the time to go on this journey with Dr. Robinson and Dr. Johnson.

—**Jor-El Godsey,** President, Heartbeat International

I first met Haywood and Noreen decades ago and have accompanied them on the intense road of healing. Now, in *The Scalpel and the Soul*, you can walk with them too. The book is not only an inspiring testimony; it is a roadmap for how our whole society can be cured of what the authors call the "cancer" of abortion. "There was nothing to do but weep," they tell us at one point. Our culture must get to that point too, so that having wept, we too will be able to embrace the freedom and joy that they did.

—**Frank Pavone,** National Director, Priests for Life

The Scalpel and the Soul is a testament to God's pursuit of man. It uncovers one family's path to God's promise of redemption and is a must read for those whose lives seem shattered by the "choice" of abortion.

—**Catherine Davis,** Founder and President,
The Restoration Project

It happened at a pro-life fund raiser at the Rio Ballroom in Las Vegas. I was the entertainer and Dr. Haywood was the keynote speaker. When he told his conversion story, I sang afterwards with tears in my eyes. I believe this book will do that for you and even more as you travel on his and Noreen's life-changing journey.

—**Leon Patillo,** Singer and Evangelist

One compelling reason to read a book is the authenticity of the author. This is an honest testimony of two physicians who, early in their careers, were abortion providers. Both experienced a transcendental 180 degree turn in their lives. With this book about what happened and why, their legacy and their spiritual transformation are written for all to see.

—**Johnny Hunter,** DD, National Director of Life Education and Resource Network

Dr. Robinson and I both grew up in South Central LA. I've known him and his late wife, Dr. Johnson, a long time. Their testimony of how Jesus transforms a person's life resonates soundly within my soul, as I have a similar experience.

—**Star Parker,** Founder and President of the Center for Urban Renewal and Education (CURE)

Thank God for two former abortion doctors who possess an unflinching courage to speak life—that precious lives might be saved.

—**Rick Rigsby,** PhD, President, Rick Rigsby Communications

There is no book like this. The dramatic story of Haywood and Noreen's life—before and after their conversion—is unprecedented. When abortion is discussed, what is usually left out are the people who do abortions, how they do it, and why they do it. This book takes you into a world you've never seen and drops you off into a hope that too many in our culture do not think is possible. A must read.

—**Shawn D. Carney,** CEO of 40 Days for Life, Bestselling Author of four books including *The Beginning of the End of Abortion* and *What to Say When: The Complete New Guide to Discussing Abortion*

Abortion supporters have long relied on abstraction to advance their bloody campaign. In *The Scalpel and the Soul,* doctors Haywood Robinson and Noreen Johnson offer an intimate and particular account of how the abortion industry really works. Their story is at times heart-rending, at others inspiring, and consistently illuminating. Their courage in writing is a powerful gift to the pro-life cause.

—**Michael Knowles,** *The Daily Wire*

The Scalpel and the Soul pierces the heart, publishes the truth, promotes a future that preserves life, and proposes a way to eternally embrace the love of God on an everyday basis.

—**Walter B. Hoye, II,** Founder and President of Issues for Life Foundation, Founder of the Frederick Douglass Foundation of California

Dr. Haywood Robinson's and Dr. Noreen Johnson's book is a monumental gift to the cause of defending life from the womb to the tomb and beyond. We are grateful.

—**Alveda King,** PhD, Founder of Speak for Life and Author of the bestseller *King Rules*

In this harrowing yet beautifully told salvation story, two former abortionists of the post-Roe era find what sinners in every age need most: redemption. *The Scalpel and the Soul* is a monument to the truth that good can burst forth from evil. Every doctor, nurse, and adult in the land should read it. This powerful book could single-handedly launch the next moral awakening.

—**Mary Eberstadt,** Senior Research Fellow at the Faith & Reason Institute

Like many doctors before them, Noreen Johnson and Haywood Robinson were trained to become abortionists and to look the other way when asked to perform such a horrible deed. *The Scalpel and the Soul* is the inspiring story of how their faith in God led them back to both the scientific and spiritual truth that abortion is a grievous wrong. It's hard to walk away from this book without marveling. If God could change their hearts and minds on abortion, surely we can trust in Him and work to change the hearts and minds of the whole nation.

—**Mollie Hemingway,** Editor in Chief of *The Federalist*

THE
SCALPEL
and the SOUL

THE
SCALPEL
and the SOUL

Our Radical Transformation as Husband and Wife Abortion Doctors

Noreen Johnson, MD, & Haywood Robinson, MD
with Cindy & David Lambert

K|A.
KOLBE & ANTHONY
PUBLISHING

The Scalpel and the Soul
Our Radical Transformation as Husband and Wife Abortion Doctors
Noreen Johnson, MD, and Haywood Robinson, MD
with Cindy and David Lambert

ISBN 978-1-7370477-5-9 (hardcover)
ISBN: 978-1-7370477-6-6 (softcover)

Cover design by Jam Graphic Design
Edited by David Lambert for Lambert Editorial

Manufactured in the United States of America

23 24 25 26 27 • 19 18 17 16 15 14 13 12 11 10 9 8 7 6 5 4 3 2 1

*In commemoration of the incalculable
number of precious lives lost, destroyed,
and sacrificed throughout millennia
due to the anti-human practice
of the shedding of innocent blood.*

Contents

Foreword

I FIRST MET DR. HAYWOOD ROBINSON AND HIS WIFE Dr. Noreen Johnson because of an eye-catching yellow Volkswagen Beetle. The family who owned the car had just moved into our neighborhood, so I stopped by to meet our new neighbors. I was greeted by a gracious woman with the prettiest smile, Haywood's mother, Mrs. Elsie Robinson. She told me that Haywood and Noreen had moved from California to Texas to establish their medical practice in Bryan/College Station, Texas. Elsie belonged to a church different from the one I pastored, but she encouraged me to meet her son and daughter-in-law to see if they would like to attend my church.

Soon thereafter, my wife and I invited Haywood and Noreen to lunch, and thus began a long and wonderful friendship. As we finished lunch that day, I felt a strong urge to tell them that God was going to use them in a mighty way in our community. They smiled kindly and graciously as I delivered that message. I can only imagine what they were thinking of such an unusual comment. Little did any of us realize that prophecy would come to pass not only in Bryan/College Station, Texas, but would spread worldwide.

In this book, you'll read about Haywood attending the Leon Patillo concert at Aldersgate Church, about Leon's challenge to those in the audience, and how Haywood responded—and how his response affected not just his own life, but Noreen's as well.

Not only did Noreen and Haywood become our good friends and our doctors—together, they delivered our first granddaughter!

As their newfound faith grew, they gave their medical practice completely to the Lord. Two doctors who had been performing abortions in California now became champions for the cause of the unborn child. In *The Scalpel and the Soul*, you'll read the precious details of the journey that has led them all over the world, speaking on behalf of the unborn. They became an integral part of 40 Days for Life, one of the most influential and effective pro-life organizations. After retiring Haywood became the director of medical affairs and education for 40 Days.

Unfortunately, Noreen passed away August 28, 2021, before this book that they had begun writing together could be published. But her legacy continues—not only in this book, but in the lives of the many children born because of her advocacy.

My prayer is that this book will help many young women and men struggling with the issue of abortion, and that it will also be an inspiration for medical professionals whose hearts may be changed!

Dr. Terry Teykl
Prayer Consultant
Former Pastor

PART I

The Threshold

CHAPTER 1

The Pain That Dies
a Slow Death

Noreen

"Dr. Johnson, perform the abortion," Haywood said.

But I couldn't. I just couldn't.

This scene was unfolding not at some abortion facility, but rather at a 40 Days for Life symposium at the Marriott Marquis in Houston, Texas, in 2019. We were on the program. Haywood, Sue Thayer, and I had been assigned the topic "Former Abortionists Speak Out." As we considered how to handle our presentation (Panel discussion? Each of us speak for fifteen minutes?) Haywood said, "Let's roleplay it. Let's just present a scene based on what goes on at an abortion facility." Sue, like Haywood and me, had once worked in the abortion industry—in her case, as a facility manager.

It would be completely unrehearsed. Haywood would be the narrator and I would be the doctor, with Sue Thayer playing the part of the facility manager. We needed a patient, so we asked a young woman attending the conference, Jessica Carpenter (whose initials—JC—I'll never forget) to act the part of the patient.

I met JC in the lobby of the hotel the day before our presentation. We were immediately drawn to each other. Like most conversations at conferences such as this, ours started with small talk. But eventually, our talk circled around to the experiences, sometimes painful, that had shaped our lives.

"Abortion isn't a remote or impersonal topic for me," JC said. "I've had four of them. I've also carried babies to term that I gave up for adoption."

"You know that I'm a former abortionist," I said.

She nodded.

"But what you don't know," I said, "is that I almost aborted my first child."

We instantly exchanged a knowing look. Common ground. We'd both stood at that same threshold—that decision-making point determining the life or death of the child we carried. And though years had passed since that moment for both of us, the memories were still painfully vivid.

The next day the conferees filed into the large conference room and found seats at the round tables set up so that they would have room for their papers, books, and laptops. There were about 120 people attending, four or five at each table, with their chairs turned toward the front so that they could see our presentation.

Haywood, Sue, and I took our places, ready for our presentation. At first, in my role as the visiting abortionist, I walked onto the elevated stage and greeted Sue, who was seated at a desk doing paperwork. At first, we were just chit-chatting: "Good morning, Sue. Does it look like a busy day? How many do you have set up for me?"

"We've got twenty today, Noreen."

"And you'll write me a check when I leave?"

"That's right. We appreciate your filling in at our facility today."

We talked casually, demonstrating for the conferees how, for the facilities and the doctors, abortion is a business transaction—not a fraught, ethical issue.

In his introduction, Haywood had encouraged the audience to interrupt our presentation at any point with questions. The first questions came during this opening dialog between Sue and me, before we'd even brought the "patient" onstage. Someone's hand shot up, and Haywood called on them.

"How could you all, as doctors who took an oath to do no harm, even start doing abortions in the first place? Didn't you understand before you even started that this was something that would take a human life?"

I did my best to answer. "Few if any doctors set out when they enter medical school to be abortion doctors. But there's a process that you go through in your studies, and then especially as an intern and resident. Maybe the best way to describe it is as *dehumanization*. Or desensitization. You don't even realize it's happening. The first time you witness an abortion as a med student, you're probably very uneasy about it. The second time, not so much.

"And throughout, you're hearing from the doctors and the more advanced residents that this is a great service we're providing, that what's being removed from the women's womb is just 'products of conception.' Products of conception. How insidiously that term strips the humanity from that fetus, even as they count out his or her little fingers and toes among the carnage to make sure they got it all. The doctor himself loses his ability to identify with another human being. In so doing, he has lost a degree of his own humanity. Just as I too, eventually, lost who I was. I became someone other than who I was intended to be. And by that time, I could no longer identify with the woman on the table—I wasn't engaging with her, wasn't even seeing her. Certainly not making eye contact. And so it was easy for me to take her baby away from her. Because I had been dehumanized, the patient had also been completely depersonalized—not just the baby but the mother as well. So the abortion was not, in the doctor's eyes, an action with moral implications. It was just a service performed to make money, like giving a haircut.

"But the Lord saved me from that," I said. "And once He saved me, I got my humanity back. I was re-humanized. Re-sensitized. I'm a new creature in Christ. My hands are washed clean of that blood."

There were other questions, but soon we moved back into our roleplaying. "Time for the first patient?" I said.

Sue said, "She's all ready for you." It wasn't our goal to playact with believable props, such as a gurney. We just wanted to verbally walk the audience through the steps. So JC walked up onto the stage and sat in a chair.

And that's when our presentation fell apart.

I stepped up to the chair and stood at JC's feet. And unlike any time I had actually performed an abortion, rather than roleplayed one, I looked into JC's eyes. And it was as if I were looking into the eyes of Jesus. I thought of His words in Matthew 25, "Whatever you did for one of the least of these, you did for me."

I froze. Absolutely motionless. In a rush of emotion, I found I loved her. I couldn't harm her. I looked into JC's eyes—and Jesus was in there. My heart blossomed with a sense of compassion that I guarantee you I never felt as a doctor actually performing abortions. It was as if Jesus Himself was asking me, *Are you going to kill this baby that's about to be born, this baby I shaped in the womb to be unlike any other person who has ever lived, this baby for whom I have a very vital plan, this baby whose name I have known since before the foundation of the world?*

Seconds dragged on and I was still unable to speak or act. Unsure what was keeping me from proceeding with the roleplay, Haywood called out, "Dr. Johnson, perform the abortion." But I still couldn't move. In fact, I was transformed. It may have been only playacting to begin with, but in that moment it became real to me. I wasn't playacting then.

And while I looked into JC's eyes, she looked back at me with real emotion, this woman I'd just met, this woman who had experienced four abortions in real life and had given up however many babies for adoption—it was real to her too. She could tell exactly what was going on with me. The two of us were communicating without words. *Are you really going to do this to me?* she was saying. *I really want my baby.*

What was happening on that stage, in that roleplay, between JC the patient and me the doctor, was exactly what those who run abortion facilities *never* want to happen between doctor and patient. We were connecting, through our eyes, through our emotions. Our hearts were getting involved. And our hearts wanted to save that baby. I had become a doctor again, not an abortionist, and I could do no harm to either of the patients on the gurney, big or very small.

There's no baby! you're thinking. *It's just a roleplay. It's make believe.*

It wasn't make believe for the four babies JC had conspired to abort. It wasn't make believe for me as I thought of what might have happened if I hadn't been talked out of an abortion back in my first year of marriage—rather than giving birth to my beloved daughter Udelle. Those were not make believe—they were real.

And JC and I, two mothers, conspired together wordlessly in that moment: We would not go ahead with this abortion, roleplayed or not, make believe or not. This abortion would not happen.

Both Haywood and the audience were becoming increasingly confused and uneasy. You could have, as the old saying goes, heard a pin drop. Finally Haywood stepped in and explained the actions that I *would* have been taking, if I were performing an abortion: "Now Dr. Johnson is going to …"

But Haywood's voice seemed to momentarily fade into

the background as I thought of all the times I'd stood at that threshold and taken a life.

"Then she'll insert the cannula and hook it up to the machine," and so on, describing each step just as if I were in fact acting them out, even though I was still just standing at JC's feet, looking into her eyes.

The skit moved on and concluded, thanks to Haywood. But for me, this was a true Damascus Road moment. In those seconds, I felt the emotional power of the damage every abortion causes. In those seconds, I felt anew the impulses and desires to help and to heal that had caused me to become a doctor in the first place.

CHAPTER 2

See One, Do One, Teach One

Noreen

"This morning we'll start abortion training," said our instructor, a third-year resident. I stood outside the operating room doors in a semicircle with my fellow first-year residents at Martin Luther King Jr./Charles R. Drew Medical Center (hereafter called King/Drew) "If you don't want to participate in this you don't have to." That was followed by mostly silence and some nervous shuffling around.

We'd all known ahead of time that today would be the day. Our chief resident had announced it a few days ago with almost identical words to give us all a few days to think about our willingness to participate. In the next few awkward moments I noticed everyone else, like me, looking around at the group, to see if anyone would back out. I wondered if some were secretly hoping someone else *would* back out, because maybe that would give others the courage to do the same. I suspect that almost every doctor-in-training is at least a little uncomfortable at the beginning with the idea of learning to perform abortions.

For a few moments, silence hung heavily in the air. Then Eloise stepped forward and said loudly, "There's no way I'm goin' into that room to kill little babies! Y'all can go if you want. This isn't why *I* signed up for medical school."

All heads snapped toward her. Eyes grew wide. Feet shuffled. One resident softly snickered, while another let out a tiny involuntary gasp. But no one said a word.

If anyone was going to decline this part of the training, it made sense that it would be Eloise, I thought. She had a reputation for being a bit eccentric. Her actions and comments often stood out.

All eyes flew back to our instructor. How would she respond?

Unruffled, she soundlessly nodded at Eloise, indicating that she was free to leave, then pushed open the OR door. Everybody else, including me, followed her into the room. I had no idea, of course, as I stepped over that threshold, what impact doing so would have on my soul.

Eloise was left standing alone, a sad yet determined look on her face. She had strength—I'll give her that—and far more wisdom that I gave her credit for at the time.

That first day of abortion training, all we did was observe. We didn't pick up any instruments, we didn't assist in any way. What I didn't realize at the time is that once you allow yourself to watch, you are already sucked in. Your desensitization has begun.

Initially, in your abortion training, you learn the first trimester procedures. These, of course, are the very early ones, so in the tissue removed, you really don't see any recognizable fetal parts. Everything has been so macerated in the suction process that it really does just look like a blob of tissue.

The strategy of those who are teaching abortion is to ease students into what, for many, is a troubling procedure. When you come back for your next session, they'll introduce you to abortions of fetuses slightly more advanced in development. At that point you're instructed to inspect everything that comes out of the suction tubing, to make sure that you're not leaving anything in the uterus that might cause problems for the patient later. So—the first week, you got somewhat acclimated to the idea of abortion because you didn't really see anything come out that looked human. Now, though, you start seeing the little fingers, a foot, an arm, a little piece of skull—and it starts to bother you more. The fetus has always *been* human, but now it starts to *look* human.

Something strange happens at this point, and I remember it very clearly from my training. At first, seeing those little identifiably human parts really bothered me—it was disturbing, even disgusting. But then, in very little time, it wasn't disturbing anymore. I could touch those little parts, move them around, count them—it was just part of the business of medicine. In a matter of only a few days, I went from thinking, *Oh, how disgusting*, to being completely desensitized to the fact that these are human parts. Until a few moments before, they were part of a unique and living human being, with DNA unlike any other person who's ever lived.

That gradual desensitization leads to rationalization,

when you start to turn the morality of abortion on its head in your mind. Eventually, you begin to see it not as terminating a human life, but rather as doing a service for women who need you. You're offering them compassion in their time of despair. You're providing for them a crucial service—one, in fact, that others are trying to prevent them from obtaining. You begin to see yourself—and you truly believe this—as their godsend. So, obviously, once you've reached that stage, what do you think of those who oppose abortion? They, like Eloise, are the oddballs. They are the enemy. Not just *your* enemy, but the enemy of your patients.

We believe the lie that these women we sell abortions to just get over it. Nothing is further from the truth. They are damaged for life. How is it that we accept that a woman grieves with a miscarriage—which is medically referred to as a spontaneous abortion—and say that there is no grief or remorse when a woman pays to have her baby killed. That's just totally inconsistent. Abortion is murder. That's why in 2004 Scott Peterson was convicted of *two* murders, not just one. (He was the California man who murdered his pregnant wife.) Sometimes society recognizes the preborn as a precious human life, but in abortion, not so. Haywood and I often refer to this as the *abortion distortion*.

Haywood

After medical school comes internship and residency. Noreen and I did ours at King/Drew in Willowbrook, an unincorporated community north of Compton and south of the Watts neighborhood of Los Angeles, not terribly far from where I grew up. King/Drew is where we first met in 1978—my first year, Noreen's second. Noreen's program—obstetrics and gynecology—required four years of residency; mine—family practice—required three. So we finished at the same time because I came to King/Drew at the end of her first year.

Among my most indelible memories of medical school is the incredible power and influence of the medical school faculty. The truth is, we quasi-idolized them. And for other reasons than just their personality or accomplishments. We knew, for instance, that they were going to write, or at least influence, our evaluations. We didn't want to alienate or fail to impress people who held that much power over our future.

The pecking order was faculty members, senior residents, and then junior residents. All of them collectively contributed to an influence on us that was so powerful. Call it "academic mob rule." Once a mob's direction is set, it sweeps everyone along with it, in directions they might never have chosen on their own, without mob influence.

I was influenced by it myself.

If you've heard the term *internship* used to describe what a doctor does next after medical school—that really just refers to your first year of residency. And in those days at King/Drew, abortion was taught during internship as part of the gynecology unit.

At King/Drew, abortions were performed on the second floor in an area called at that time 2-I. This is the site where interns were initiated into the abortion culture. Abortion training would take place weekly. As an intern, as low on the residency totem pole as you can get, you might be taught by a third-year resident, or even a second year.

Now if the intern has reservations about abortion, then once the attending physician has assured him it's all right, even best for the patient, and the senior resident has said the same thing, what is the intern supposed to think—or do?

All it takes is stepping over the threshold into the OR in 2-I and witnessing your first abortion without protest. At that point, you've become a willing participant in the abortion culture. Before we entered the room, the resident we were following would say, "This is really no big deal. It's just another D&C."

But it wasn't! An abortion is performed with the specific intent of deliberately terminating the life of the child. Doctors are meant to be healers. And deep inside, I must have known that. But my view of abortion was pretty much the same as my view of other medical procedures we were taught, by which I mean, I was practical rather than moral, and I followed the lead of my instructors.

I can't overstate how much courage it would have taken to stand there in the hallway outside the room where abortions were performed, and say, "No, I won't do it." So my hat is off to Noreen's classmate, Eloise. You desperately want to obtain your medical license, and this faculty could make you or break you. The last thing you want to do is rock the boat. What you want is the best grade and the best evaluation, and the evaluation is predominantly subjective. You take comprehensive, standardized tests, of course, but in the end whether you get your license depends on what these attending physicians think of you. If you stand out, you want it to be for your hard work and brilliant insights—not for resisting their guidance and implying that their position on abortion is morally and ethically suspect. Most of the faculty were liberal in their politics and social worldview. If you're conservative, you really can't say in class what you would like to say—they won't tolerate it. And your grade may be in jeopardy.

When patients would come in for abortions, stamped on the front of their charts in bold red ink would be "VIP," meaning Voluntary Interruption of Pregnancy. Notice the word *interruption* rather than the more accurate *termination*. The death culture has a penchant for euphemisms that glorify and paint in a positive light the horrors of abortion. We would see the patients, examine them, find out their gestational age, and then schedule them for abortion. Roe v. Wade had passed in 1973, just five years before, so in many ways it was a new procedure.

One of the most noticeable things for me about the procedure was that no one was interacting with the patient. It was completely impersonal, and obviously the doctors there wanted to keep it that way. Everybody was acting so matter of fact! And definitely, nobody was grieving. We tend to take our cues on behavior and attitude and even emotion from our elders—from those who are higher up than we are in one way or another. So when you watch your first abortion as an intern, you watch the doctors and older residents for cues—how should I react? And then you observe a second abortion, this time consciously patterning your response after the responses you saw from the doctors—matter of fact, professional, clinical.

So as an intern, the next step comes during the following abortion session: They sit you down on that stool and it's your turn to do one.

In a hospital setting, abortions were usually performed under IV sedation with medicines like Valium. For your first abortion, the patient would already have been placed on the exam table, examined, and sedated. You insert the speculum. Then you take the tenaculum, grasp the cervix, and inject local anesthesia around it. Then you take the dilator and open the mouth of the cervix. Then you insert the suction curette into the uterus and turn it on. When that's done, you've done the abortion. It takes ten minutes or less.

Okay—finished? You're in with us now, says the unspoken reality. *You're initiated.*

And so, one by one, we were indeed initiated.

We each had done our first abortion. Even if you came that day with a resistance to the idea of abortion, now you had done one. The second one would be less objectionable.

Similarly, the medical faculty was reassured by the willingness of each intern to perform that first abortion. Now, we couldn't condemn what they were doing without condemning ourselves, because we too had ended a human life. We were complicit.

Even if you refused to do abortions, we learned, there was one more way by which the medical profession would seek to make you complicit. When a patient was interested in obtaining an abortion, even if your practice did not offer them, you were expected to refer that patient to another doctor or facility that *would* perform an abortion. And this isn't just some minor preference that most other doctors *hope* you will do. According to the code of ethics of the American College of Obstetricians and Gynecologists, it's unethical to not refer a patient to an abortion provider if they request it.

In medical training, there is a saying: "See one, do one, teach one," which refers to the method by which medicine is learned. In her first year, Noreen had seen her first abortion and had done her first abortion. In her second year—my first—it was her turn to teach interns how to perform an abortion, and it just so happened that Noreen was one of my abortion instructors.

For each of us as individuals, our mission as physicians, as we saw it, was to follow the Hippocratic Oath written thousands of years ago that forbids abortion, sexual relations with patients, and euthanasia, and that maintains confidentiality. A corollary to this is "first do no harm" or "primun non nocere." How is it that in that ancient time, without technology or even pregnancy tests, these lofty esteemed values could be adopted? They simply recognized the sanctity of human life and the value of protecting that life, from conception to natural death. At the time Noreen was teaching me, we saw no disparity between performing abortions and the responsibility of preserving life. And we never would have guessed that performing abortions would forge a partnership between us. Neither would we have ever dreamed that such a quick and noncomplex procedure had the power to take such a toll on our souls.

All that was yet to come.

CHAPTER 3

Moonlighting

Haywood

Despite how busy all we residents were, I still had eyes in my head, and I began to notice, with more than casual interest, one of the other residents. And one of the first things I noticed, other than that she was beautiful, was that she was very neat. Her scrubs always seemed as if they had been tailored (no small feat with scrubs) and they were always tucked in just right. Her hair was styled perfectly, too. She was proper.

But what sealed the deal for me was when she opened her mouth and I heard that Trinidadian accent for the first time. I listened in amazement—it was like music. *This lady's really got it going on,* I thought.

Her name, I found out, was Noreen Johnson. We were both on the same team—the Blue Team. Noreen was in OBGYN and I was in family practice, but all of us trained in abortion.

My mother met her fairly early in my residency. In those days, security and regulations weren't as big an issue as they are now, and no one cared if my mother came to the hospital to watch her son in action as a resident. She loved watching her doctor son deliver a baby. So I invited my mother to spend an entire shift on labor and delivery. The other residents loved it, because any time my mother went anywhere, she brought food. Tuna salad sandwiches … cookies … oh, those cookies! …her special-recipe punch …

Word would go out like magic, and soon the rest of the residents were dropping by wherever my mom's food was set out. Meanwhile, my mom was wandering through the ward, giving advice to the new moms: "Well, make sure you do this and that."

Some time later, once the romance had been kindled, Noreen and I came to Mama's apartment—my mother and father had separated sometime between when I was in undergraduate school and medical school—and after Noreen left, I said, "Well, Mama. I think I've met the one."

She just smiled and said, "You know, when I met her in the hospital, I thought you might wind up with her." What was amazing about that was, when she met Noreen in the hospital, we hadn't begun any kind of romantic relationship or even a social one. But Mama took note and kept Noreen in her heart.

Noreen

One of my best friends during my residency was Brad, a Jewish guy married to an Ethiopian woman. He was my next-door neighbor in Redondo Beach, where I rented an apartment. It isn't just that Brad and I were close—our lives intersected in many ways besides being next-door neighbors. We looked out for each other. We were also residents together at King/Drew.

Haywood had been scheduled to go on a trip to the SNMA (Student National Medical Association) Conference, which was being held that year in Hartford, Connecticut. My friend, Gail Jackson, MD, was to attend as well. However, two weeks before they were to leave, Gail broke her leg, and Haywood asked me to go along instead. As long as I was going to be flying, I scheduled a stop after the conference to rendezvous with my boyfriend who was studying in Rochester at Mayo Clinic College of Medicine and Science. I found it challenging managing a long-distance relationship, and my feelings for my boyfriend had been wavering a bit. I wanted to see if being together would rekindle some of the romance.

Haywood kindly picked me up from my apartment on his way to the airport. As we left my apartment, Haywood was carrying my suitcase. In my hand was my per diem check so I could cover expenses on the trip. But the name on it was incorrect. It was addressed to Dr. Noreen Robinson! Haywood's check was correct: Dr. Haywood Robinson. We laughed about it. (What a prescient slip-up on someone's part!) Brad poked his head out of his apartment's front door and saw us leaving. He could hardly contain his suspicious grin, watching from his doorway. I considered stopping to explain what was really going on—just a professional trip for two colleagues—but we were pressed for time, so I didn't, no doubt leaving Brad's imagination running wild.

On the flight out of Los Angeles, Haywood and I couldn't stop talking. We were upgraded to first class—a first for me. Over drinks and snacks, we enjoyed great conversation—so great that, at the hotel, not yet finished talking, we went to relax in the Jacuzzi. And even after that, we continued to talk way past midnight.

We worked together the next day at the SNMA Conference, talked again over dinner—again until late into the night. The next day—same thing, until it was time to depart for home.

At the airport, my flight departed ahead of his. As we said goodbye, we embraced for the first time, and we could tell we were falling in love. "I'll pick you up at the airport when you get back to LA," Haywood said softly into my ear before letting me go. All of a sudden, I was no longer looking forward to this side visit to see my boyfriend—unsure of what I felt, and of what I would say. Instead, I could hardly wait to return to Los Angeles.

Our relationship grew fast and furious. I avoided phone calls from my boyfriend—but I couldn't avoid him forever, because he was planning to move to Los Angeles! When he arrived there and started showing up at my door, I wouldn't answer, afraid of what I would have to tell him.

Finally, he intercepted me while I was on call at the hospital. Looking me directly in the eye he said, "I know there's someone else in your life—has to be, or else why won't you talk to me? So whoever it is, you'd better get rid of him. I'm here now. So he's got to go."

After the weeks of dreading this conversation, I was surprised at how calm I was when I said, "If anyone has to go, it's you."

He turned and walked away without a word.

Haywood and I were inseparable thereafter. He lived in the dorm for interns and residents, but pretty soon he was mostly visiting his dorm room and spending much of his time at my plush, two-bedroom apartment in Fox Hills, near Marina del Rey, where I had moved from Redondo Beach. My friend Brad, when I moved away from Redondo Beach, decided he liked the area where I had settled better and moved near me in Fox Hills.

You have to work one year after medical school to get a license. And you can't work in the real world until you have a license. To get that license, you have to pass a test at the end of that first year—part three of the United States Medical Licensing Exam or the National Board Exam. So the minute that you pass one of these exams you apply for your license, and once you get it you can work anywhere in the state.

Because I began my residency a year before Haywood did, when we met I was already licensed. But just because you have your license to practice medicine, that doesn't mean you're suddenly rolling in money. In fact, you don't make much as a resident. Even so, once I'd been licensed, I grew curious as to how it was that another resident, Drew, could always afford such expensive things. He not only had a fancy and expensive sports car, he had already bought his first house! "Brad," I asked my neighbor one day, "where does Drew get the money to buy such lovely things? Is he from a rich family?"

"Easy money for him," he said. "Through abortions. He moonlights. If you're interested, I can tell you how to go about it."

"Well—let's hear it," I said.

Brad told me about an abortion facility in Hollywood, and very soon I was doing abortions there once or twice a week. I was paid thirty dollars per abortion, in cash. This was 1979, when thirty dollars was quite a sum of money. A McDonald's hamburger cost thirty-eight cents then, and a gallon of gas cost about eighty-five cents. I pocketed the cash, never guessing that I'd just been smitten with another romance. And that was just the beginning.

There were a multitude of abortion facilities throughout Southern California. You could make a lot of money in just a few hours. The abortion itself cost the patient maybe a hundred and fifty dollars back then.

Obviously, if you're being paid per abortion, then the more you do, the more you earn. You start priding yourself in how efficient you can become at it, how quickly you can get each one done and move on to the next.

I got better and better at it, faster and faster, and pretty soon word began to get around. An abortion facility that was owned and run by women contacted me. They were specifically looking for female doctors because there weren't that many of us doing abortions back then, and the women who ran the facility, Maureen and Corey and Carrie, felt that women were more compassionate, better able to identify with the female patients, than male doctors. Soon I was working for them too. More nights a week equals more money. The romance was growing in intensity. And on a Saturday, they would line up about thirty or forty abortions for me to do, one after the other, all day long. Besides that, the women at the new facility paid me more—*fifty* dollars per abortion. Doesn't sound like much by today's standards, but remember, this was 1979. And if I did forty abortions on a weekend at fifty dollars each, I would walk home with two thousand dollars in cash. In 1979.

I know—this all sounds pretty greedy and mercenary. Didn't we become doctors to help people live better, healthier lives? Yes! That was why I was completing my medical education, and that's why I was looking forward to building my own OBGYN practice one day. But that's not why I was moonlighting in an abortion facility. What drives abortion facilities is the money. *It is a business that is all about money.*

What other incentive would there be? In truth, doctors as a whole don't *like* to do abortions. Why would they? It is gruesome work. There's nothing nice about it, except for the fact that the money's good.

One day, however, I had an abortion patient who seemed particularly troubled before and after her procedure. I spoke to the facility director afterward. "I'm not sure I just did that woman a favor," I said. "I could tell as soon as I walked into the room that the patient was, at the very least, of two minds about going ahead with the abortion."

"She'll be fine," the director said. "It's natural to be nervous before—"

"I know that," I said, "but isn't it possible that some of the women who come here for abortions are coerced to have this procedure—either from family members or from social or economic factors?"

"I'm sure some of them are," she replied, "but it's not our job to sort that out for them. We provide an important service. There's no way we can know or pass judgment on whether each of our patients is making the best choice about whether or not to take advantage of that service. The patients have to take responsibility for that choice themselves."

As reasonable as that sounded, it was, I know now, incomplete and self-serving. How many women step into an abortion facility wishing they could have just said no to the irresponsible boyfriend or angry parent who insisted they come, or wishing that they had found other ways to overcome the dire financial straits that had convinced them they just couldn't support one more hungry mouth? Imagine the difference it might have made in such a woman's life— and the life of her baby—if instead of proceeding with the abortion, I had taken her hand and said, "You don't have to do this. There are other options, and I can send you somewhere equipped to tell you about them." How many women would have taken that potential way out? I know beyond the shadow of a doubt that many of them would have—because working in the pro-life movement, we've met them, talked to them. And heard their enthusiastic words of thanks.

And seen the pride on their faces as they held up their little ones.

By the time I was offered a second abortion job in downtown LA, I figured that Haywood and I could spend more time together if he also performed abortions. He already knew the basics of the procedure. He just needed to learn certain tips and tricks specific to a quick evacuation of an intact pregnancy. Haywood liked the idea of making extra money as well as working with me, so he gladly signed on.

The owners, seeing great potential for profit, decided to open another facility in Orange County and offered me the position of medical director. Haywood and I were the only doctors working at that facility. We would drive down to Orange County together twice during the week and again on Saturdays to perform abortions.

Christmas Eve, 1980. I was on call at King/Drew that night—just because the rest of the world has a holiday and has the evening off doesn't mean medical personnel do. There was nothing unusual about that. This part *was* unusual, though: Haywood insisted that I not drive myself home from work at the end of my shift. He wanted to pick me up Christmas Day.

So he drove to King/Drew in his VW. It wasn't surprising that he was playing music, but it was very quickly obvious that this was a special mixtape that he, being the DJ and romantic that he is, had prepared specially for our drive home. I still remember the first song, "Someday at Christmas," by Stevie Wonder. When we arrived at the apartment, the music continued inside. I started to sit down on the couch, but he asked if, first, I would get the two glasses out of the refrigerator.

They were chilled champagne glasses—and sitting in one was a beautiful ring with a pear-shaped diamond.

Tears streaming down my face, I said, "Oh, Haywood!"

Of course he had set up a recorder to capture the moment. We embraced, cried, and danced slowly to the Stevie Wonder song, "You and I." Clearly Stevie Wonder was Haywood's favorite artist.

We were married on July 18, 1981, in the church where Haywood had grown up. It was beautiful. Haywood had somehow convinced my father, who had sworn that he would never return to the US after experiencing an unusually cold winter, to come anyway and give me away. Drew, our fellow resident, was one of the groomsmen, and Brad's wife one of the bridesmaids. The reception was lavish, held in a garden theatre, with an abundance of food, drink, and dancing.

If that sounds expensive, it was. And even without the wedding, our living expenses were significant. We lived, remember, in Los Angeles, consumption capital of the country and one of the most expensive places to live. And we loved every part of that, and everything it implied. But compared to many of our friends, even those who like us were doctors, we were doing quite well financially. Why? Because of the income we made from abortions.

From '73 (with the passing of Roe v. Wade) until the early '80s, abortion facilities in Southern California multiplied rapidly. They weren't large or even sophisticated. Most were essentially storefronts, usually in a strip mall. And they didn't advertise their presence—no writing on the windows, for instance. Little signage. The one we served was in Santa Ana, on Tustin Avenue, a largely Hispanic area. I've forgotten the actual name of it.

Haywood and I didn't start or own the facility in Santa Ana, of course. We simply came, performed the abortions, and left. If a potential investor knew an administrator or someone who knew how to run a business, they could just open an abortion facility. You could easily find the doctors to do the actual work. It worked simply: Interested medical residents, after their normal working hours or on the weekends, were part of a network. Word would get out—which abortion facilities needed coverage? And you would create relationships with those whose location or other details worked for you. Residents could also pick up abortion work from doctors in the community who, when they were busy doing other surgeries, such as hysterectomies, would farm out the abortions to residents. Sometimes we residents could leave the hospital early enough to make appointments at the facilities for abortions at 3:30 or 4 o'clock. And on the weekend, we would start accepting appointments at 9:00 or 10:00.

The Santa Ana facility wasn't elaborate. It had two entrances so that we could enter without having to pass through the reception room. We almost always worked there at the same time—but if only one of us was there, it would have been me, since I was the OBGYN. The facility had two employees: a nurse and someone to run the front office, collect cash, sign patients in, and do whatever needed doing. The nurse assisted and laid out on the Mayo stand (the metal stand that held the instruments for the current procedure), before each abortion, all of the instruments we needed for that abortion: the long-needled syringe for injecting the anesthetic, speculum, cervical dilators, tenaculum, forceps, curette, and miscellaneous others.

No one, when they enter medical school, aspires to be an abortionist. They have other goals—to be a cardiologist, or an internist, or a neurosurgeon, or a family practitioner. Abortion is something that happens along the way, quite often, in our observation, as a way to make money. Maybe it starts as a way to pay off medical school loans, as it did for us, but for too many, if it continues, it does so as a way to pay off a boat. Consider these questions: Have you ever seen a free abortion facility? Or met a medical missionary abortionist? I have not ever seen an abortion practice in any context other than as a money-making venture.

Now that's not to say that certain circumstances may not lure a doctor into performing *a particular or occasional* abortion for other reasons. In fact, I'll share later in the book two such circumstances I faced. There may be times when a doctor believes that doing an abortion will genuinely "help" their patient under difficult circumstances. (The patient obviously being the mother, not the baby.) Or there may be times when doctors are made aware that a patient is definitely going to abort, perhaps in an unsafe manner, and determines that if the abortion is going to happen anyway the doctor would rather do it themselves knowing it will be done as safely as possible for the mother. But this is when a doctor must rely on the principles and the Hippocratic Oath and the fact that they are meant to be healers, not executioners. Since every abortion is meant to be fatal to the baby, even when tempted to perform an abortion, doctors need to hold fast to their understanding that an abortion is outside of their rightful place.

There are abortion specialists, of course, some of them very well known. Such as LeRoy Carhart, MD, in Maryland, who specializes in late-term abortions. He's in his eighties. Some of them do abortions as late as thirty-two weeks. And there is formal training available for that, beyond the training we residents receive which we described above. The American College of Obstetricians and Gynecologists (ACOG) offers a one-year fellowship focusing on late-term/third trimester abortions that can be added on to the regular four-year OBGYN fellowship.

Why is ACOG offering this training in late-term abortions? Because there are fewer and fewer of the existing doctors who offer it. It is the most gruesome work. The few still doing them are older, some of them past seventy. ACOG wants to offer that specialized training to keep newer doctors filling the pipeline. Think about this. The size and gestational age of the babies whose lives are being taken in those late-term abortions is greater than those in the neonatal intensive care unit where tremendous efforts are being made to save babies' lives.

Haywood

I have a particular memory related to the years we spent doing abortions. I had completed an abortion and had a brief break before the next. The nurse who'd been assisting me had stayed with the patient a little longer than I had, then joined me for a break. She seemed a little troubled, so I asked if everything was okay.

"It's just that the patient asked me a question after you left," she said. "She was lying on the table, staring up at the ceiling. Quietly, so I almost couldn't hear her, she said, 'Was it a boy or a girl? The baby.'"

The nurse paused for a moment, then said, "I've been asked that same question more than once. It always makes me a little sad."

The reason that memory keeps coming back to me is what it reveals about the patient's attitude. By that time the baby is gone. All the mutilated body parts have been taken away. But there lies a woman with a mother's heart. Maybe she didn't even want to be there—she might have come because she was pressured to, or because she felt that she had no choice. She might have felt abandoned or unsupported. She might have yearned for someone to rescue her. Regardless of why she was there, if she asked that question, she must have been looking for closure. She wanted the ability to envision the little life that was lost so that she could bid it goodbye. It humanizes the moment.

And the minutes after an abortion are definitely a moment that needs humanizing.

Was it a boy or a girl?

The thing is, a *boy* or a *girl* isn't just a lump of protoplasm, a glob of tissue. A boy or a girl is a person. Someone whose coming might have been joyously anticipated by someone. A boy or a girl is destined to have a unique future.

Yet somehow, despite the jarring words of the nurse and my discomfort with them, when our break was over we went back into the abortion chamber and invaded and emptied the womb of another woman. My reasoning and conscience never took the next step. Neither she nor I asked the logical next questions: *Could it be that destroying these little lives is wrong? That it's the wrong thing for the mother as well as the baby? And that it was the wrong thing for the doctor to do in the first place?*

Shame on us! We sold out at the cost of millions of lives. Doctors should have never accepted the role of executioners when Roe v. Wade was passed. Doctors could have shouted a collective *"No!"* We could have insisted that abortion is not medicine and pregnancy is not a disease. But we cowered to the prevailing voices of the day and lost our moral footing. Just as Noreen and I were romanced by the dollars lining our pockets.

All of this makes me think that it isn't really compassion those in the world of abortion feel for the women in their care, even though they sometimes speak words that indicate compassion. I think it's false compassion. I think the words of compassion come because, despite our best efforts to keep the patients at arm's length and not engage with them personally, sometimes it happens anyway. Maybe the patient reaches out to you or a colleague directly, as the woman did in the nurse's story I just told, and when that happens, you have to respond somehow. So you put on your best bedside manner and you react in a way that sounds compassionate. Even if you're about to scrub up and go into the next room for the next abortion.

Back in the days when Noreen and I were doing abortions, there were very few places offering alternatives.

Nowadays, there are thousands of pregnancy resource centers (PRCs) equipped with ultrasound equipment enabling mothers to see their preborn children and eager to give out supplies and clothing. There are maternity homes, adoption agencies, and other choices that, if they were available at all in the 1980s, were available in far smaller numbers and perhaps not locally.

Ultrasound machines are one of the most significant life-saving tools of our time. Abortion-prone women, when shown an ultrasound of their child, change their mind and give birth 80 percent of the time. That's why PRCs are so hated by the abortion industry. Babies lives are saved, which means abortion revenue goes down.

These days, PRCs outnumber abortion facilities six to one.

Six to one.

Our challenge, then, is to woo more parents who are facing unexpected pregnancies to step inside a PRC and see for themselves the tiny baby snuggled inside the womb. In that moment, so very often, a new romance is kindled—the love between parent and child.

CHAPTER 4

From the Playboy Club to Reality

Haywood

I'd like to be able to say that my initial day of abortion training in my first year of residency was my first up close and personal encounter with abortion, but that wouldn't be honest. The truth is that I'd had an encounter a few years before that—an encounter about which I feel great remorse. In fact, that's not my only regret of the young man that I was.

I never took a pause in my education. I had a few weeks off between high school and college, and only three or four weeks between college and starting medical school in 1974 at University of California, Irvine (UCI). It was a very new campus, built on a massive parcel of land donated by the Irvine family. It was only partly completed when I began—

the circular part known as Aldrich Park and the buildings surrounding it, plus some dorms and apartments. There was a lot of empty land on campus in those days, but that changed fast. When I went to my twenty-year class reunion, I got lost on campus, it had changed so much.

When I graduated from medical school, on one hand I was a wonderfully social extrovert, and on the other, I had an underdeveloped conscience. So my social life looked like just what you might expect from a young man who liked to hang out, party, and take advantage of women—and then move on, with no sense of responsibility for what he'd done. I'm not proud of that. I could, truthfully, say "Everybody was doing it," at least among my acquaintances. But that, of course, is no excuse.

Nor was that lifestyle a new thing for me. Flash back to my undergrad years at California Institute of Technology (Caltech) in Pasadena, California.

I was seeing a girl, Sharon, but I didn't consider it to be serious. That doesn't mean I wasn't nudging her toward sexual intimacy if I sensed that she was open to it.

We had been out one evening and when we returned to campus, we gravitated toward my dorm room. She was looking especially attractive that night, and I was expecting some intimacy. Instead, she seemed distant, didn't return my caresses, and was not at all talkative—until, that is, she said, "Haywood—I'm pregnant."

I said nothing—because I was speechless. And scared.

Considering that everything in my life at that point was about me, what her pregnancy meant for me was that I had a problem I had to solve before it got in the way of my plans and goals. There was no way I was going to try to get through medical school and the hard years of residency with a wife and baby holding me back. I didn't even see how it could be done. Would I have to work long hours each week to earn enough to support a family? Just give up on medical school and my goal of becoming a doctor? I was focused on me and me alone. Nothing was going to stand in the way of me and my life goals.

I doubted very much that Sharon would be open to the idea of an abortion. But the thoughts running constantly through my mind weren't, "Should I think about keeping this baby?" but rather "How am I going to get out of this?"

I took a few days to think it over, and then when we spoke next, I told her, "There's no way we can do this. I don't have a job. And you—you're still living at home. How would we ever afford a place to live, food, and everything else?"

The fact that she was living at home was only half the problem—the rest was the home she was living in. Her parents were great, really—aside from the fact that her daddy was a Pentecostal preacher. He led a little storefront church, which didn't pay him much, so he drove a school bus to make ends meet. If his daughter got pregnant, would a scandalized congregation insist that he give up his church?

"Maybe we should go to counseling," I said.

We did, but only once. The psychologist was an acquaintance of mine on staff at Caltech. I did most of the talking, giving my point of view—*I'm studying to become a doctor, I have no income*, blah blah blah. Poor Sharon, all she could really manage to say was, "Well, I don't really want to get an abortion." The counselor listened to both of us, and in the end he sided with me. We conspired and bullied her. It was shameful.

At the time, he said that he didn't really have any good alternatives to offer. If we were having that conversation today, he could have sent us to a pregnancy resource center. There we would have heard the pros and cons about all the possible options available to us—keeping the baby, creating an adoption plan, which agencies could help us and in what way, and so on. But at the time, there were only a couple of options, at least that were known to poor college students: a few places you could get an abortion (because of the Roe v. Wade decision) and homes for unwed mothers, which carried a stigma. Even just the thought of telling her conservative preacher daddy was daunting.

She walked out of that meeting seeing clearly that she had no support—not from me, and not from the counselor either. Tragically, that story can be told by thousands upon thousands of women who find themselves on the abortion table when they really don't want to be there. Their physiology is programmed for love, nurturing and protecting, not harming their child. Yet they are persuaded or, worse yet, bullied or even forced to end the life of their child because they feel alone with no alternatives.

One of the few places abortions were offered locally was a hospital in Bel Air, almost thirty miles away. I had no car—I don't think I even had a driver's license. I had a friend, accompanied by his girlfriend, drive us to the hospital. I remember all of us sitting in the car as my friend drove us there, then we three waited in the car while she went in, alone, to have the abortion.

It seems callous and insensitive now that I didn't go in with her, to at least wait with her and offer what support I could. And no doubt it was. But at the time no one knew what the protocol was for accompanying someone to an abortion. Allow them their privacy? Stay with them till that last possible moment? So I did nothing. I let her go through it alone.

After what seemed like a couple of hours, she came back to the car. I had thought she might experience some grief from the loss of the baby, and she might well have been feeling that inside, but mostly what she talked about was the physical pain. Maybe she didn't have a good paracervical block. But it's also true that, if you're feeling any emotional pain, that will amplify your physical pain. She said, "It was a ripping sensation. It felt like they were just tearing the insides out of me."

Then we drove back to Caltech. There wasn't a whole lot of talking in the car. Maybe we stopped and my friend and I got something to eat—I'm sure Sharon had no appetite. She was obviously feeling some physical pain, and no doubt some emotional pain as well. What was I feeling? Relief. All of my plans had been threatened, and now that threat had been removed.

I don't remember us ever talking about the abortion again.

Sharon and I were still boyfriend-girlfriend after that, but she moved to Oakland soon thereafter. We kept in touch— not so easy in those days before cell phones—but the romantic side of the relationship faded away with the distance. We wrote to each other. And she came to my graduation from medical school—not to rekindle the old romantic relationship, but just out of friendship.

I wish I could say I learned something from the experience, and that I became more sexually responsible, but no—I continued to follow the moral pattern of the day. I was happy that she'd had the abortion because that allowed me to keep my freedom. Abortion definitely affects the father as well as the mother—but many men, younger or older, don't grasp just how it affects them morally or emotionally. All they see is that abortion eliminated something that interfered with their life. They keep it at arm's length emotionally and just move on. They think of it as collateral damage. Or at best, something that's sad but necessary.

Did I ever try to come up with a solution for Sharon and me in which the baby lives? No, I didn't. There were two simple options: The baby is born—or not. If the baby is born, that puts me at a level of responsibility that I just don't want. Plus, it raises a question that's uncomfortable for me: *Am I going to have to marry Sharon now? I like Sharon, but not enough to marry her.*

When I met Noreen, I knew I'd met the right one. But I never thought of Sharon in that way. I thought of her as just a girlfriend. And when she became pregnant because of our sexual relationship, it was an unwanted complication. My way of thinking was, *We've got to get this complication fixed—and abortion is just the thing to fix this bump in the road.*

It's always risky to point out gender differences—no sooner do you try than someone yells out, "Sexist!" But I'm going to do it anyway because I think this is accurate. In questions of relationships and family, men tend to see things from a less emotional and more problem-solving perspective. A man thinks, *Okay, here's a problem. So we've got to find a solution to that problem. The best solution is the one that creates the fewest complications. So let's get that done—and then once it's done, what's next? Bring on the next problem!* Men don't have a tendency to spend a lot of time agonizing over the decision once we've made it. The decision's made. It's done. So, let's move on.

After an abortion, while the man has moved on and is now thinking about his car that has broken down and that he doesn't have money to fix, the woman is grieving her child. Her partner wonders when she's going to finally get over it. *Let's move on.*

Men tend to look at an abortion as something that repairs a playtoy. Let's get this fixed, and we'll be back to having fun in no time. That sounds crass—but sadly, it's how many men look at it. *Have your abortion. It's the best thing for both of us. Then—do you need a few days of quiet time? Okay. Now— you over it? Great. Wanna go to the club? Or the beach? How about a movie?*

Is what I just described an oversimplified, stereotypical male response to the problem? Sure. Are there lots of nuances in the way any particular man may respond? Yes. Some respond beautifully. But I believe there are some biologically built-in differences in how men and women respond to abortion.

And speaking of stereotypical responses: What about the cliché offered by many men: "Well, whatever you decide, I'll support you." Isn't that just another way of saying, "You're on your own"? I never offered that to Sharon because my fear was that she would say, "Okay, well—in that case, I'll keep the baby and we'll just figure out the practical implications of that when they arise." If she'd said that, I'd have thought, *Oh, no—now I'm going to be partially responsible.* Partially responsible? In a committed relationship about to bring a new baby into the family, there's no room for either partner to be thinking about being *partially responsible.* You're all in.

Fast forward now to the latter part of my senior year at Caltech. 1974. I have one brother, a twin, Howard. One night Howard and I and one of our friends were out, and both of them had brought their girlfriends. Somehow we all wound up at someone's house. Howard had decided to set me up with someone for the evening. She came to the house, and that's how I met Robin. There was drinking, there was dancing, and at the end of the evening we decided to exchange phone numbers and maybe see each other again.

We went on a date, this time a double date with a guy I admired who was executive director of the Y at Caltech and his wife. He was a mentor to me and a great friend. And where did we choose to go on this date? The Playboy Club.

There are no longer any Playboy Clubs; the chain went belly-up long ago. But they weren't strip clubs, as you might imagine. They were in fact high-class restaurants and night-clubs with top-name entertainment. The main thing they had connecting them to *Playboy Magazine*, other than the logo, was that the meals and drinks were served by waitresses and barmaids wearing the stereotypical bunny costume and ears. We went to the one near Beverly Hills. Everything was first class.

Did our choice of date location have anything to do with what came after? Frankly, I don't think so. The truth is, I'd never needed a visit to the Playboy Club to tend toward nudging a date in an intimate direction. All I needed was hormones. And sure enough, this date ended in bed.

As will happen, Robin got pregnant. When she told me, I didn't really offer any support. She opted not to abort. I may have seen her once during the pregnancy. She called me on the phone after she delivered—I hadn't even known that she had gone into labor. She just said, "You have a daughter. Her name is Kaishauna Lashae."

Oddly enough, after she said it, I said, "Oh! Kaishauna. K-A-I-S-H-A-U-N-A," spelling it correctly even though I'd never even heard the name before.

I went to see Robin and the baby at Kaiser Sunset, a big hospital on Sunset Boulevard in the Hollywood area. That may have been the high point in terms of my involvement in Kaishauna's childhood. I visited them very infrequently after that. I could use as an excuse that I didn't have a car. I could take a bus to get *to* LA, but once I got there it was hard to get around unless Howard was available to drive me.

On my occasional visits, Robin and I never really bonded. We'd slept together before we really got to know each other. We never really had a relationship other than sexual. We never fell in love. And now she had a baby with my DNA that I wasn't supporting.

My relationship with my daughter Kaishauna wasn't

much better. At first I would send birthday cards and so on. Pretty remote. Once I started making some money as a resident, I made some effort to support Kaishauna with school expenses and clothing and Christmas gifts. But money is a poor substitute for time and love, and I didn't offer either of those less tangible contributions.

When Sharon had gotten pregnant, I'd wanted her to have an abortion. But my thought at the time was, *If she doesn't, then I'm going to be responsible for this baby! That's going to mess up my plans!* To my shame, I really didn't have that same sense of responsibility when Robin got pregnant. There was no possibility that my "plans" were going to be messed up—I wouldn't allow it. Why was that? A large part of it was that Robin and I just never had a relationship. By the time I took Robin to the Playboy Club, I thought of myself as a player, as a guy who could get some action. And now I take a woman out one time and suddenly there's a *baby* in the picture? What kind of luck is that? If you want to think of that as the height of irresponsibility, you'd be right—and it's an irresponsibility that's rampant in our society and growing worse.

Promiscuity leads to a constellation of symptoms. Abortion is one. Absentee fathers. Deadbeat dads. Kids growing up without adequate financial resources. Welfare families. Kids who never develop any emotional closeness with a parent (or two). Those symptoms are tightly interlocked, and they contribute to each other in a self-perpetuating downward spiral. This spiral is particularly evident in the world of juvenile delinquents and prisoners where growing up without a father and without a strong male role model is incredibly common.

Robin chose to not have an abortion—certainly he right choice at the time. Despite my attitude and conduct, Kaishauna is compassionate, intelligent, wise, and beautiful inside and out. She's not only a viable, productive member of society, but she too is a physician—imagine that. I'm so proud of her. Most importantly, we've reconciled and she is a much beloved member of my family. She's a wife, the mother of my only biological grandchildren, and the grandmother of my only great grandchild. Kaishauna is my "firstborn" … because Robin made the right choice. The brave choice. I applaud her for stepping up and being the only adult in the room.

Noreen

Haywood and I got pregnant on our honeymoon.

We spent that honeymoon at a medical conference in Atlanta, Georgia, and that's where, to our surprise, we conceived. My menstrual cycles had always been regular, and being a gynecologist, well versed in natural family planning, I had timed our wedding date around the "safe period" of my menstrual cycle. Frankly, I hadn't even been connecting in my mind the thought of sex in our marriage with the thought of getting pregnant. We'd just gotten married, for Pete's sake. I shouldn't even be susceptible to impregnation at this time of the month. Should I?

Now you would think that I, as a gynecologist, would have a pretty good idea about how to prevent pregnancy, right? And I *did* want to prevent it, because as I had told Haywood before we got married, "I don't want any children." And why didn't I want children? Because we were all about money. Kids cost money, and they take up time you could spend making money. Selfish as we were, we had no room in our lives for children. God, of course, was laughing. Man proposes, and God disposes. He knew what was coming.

Haywood, by the way, didn't believe me about not wanting kids. He said, "The biological clock will tick, and you'll realize it's now or never."

When I found out I was pregnant, my first thought was, *I'll just get an abortion.* The next was, *What will Haywood think?* If I aborted a baby we'd conceived together—wouldn't he be angry with me?

So I gathered my courage and talked to Haywood about it. I cycled through the confusion of thoughts that had been running through my mind: why it was bad timing, how it would limit us. Plus I reminded him that, as I'd told him previously, I did not want children. He listened, nodded, paused—and then said quietly, "I never said *I* didn't want children." He waited a few minutes more, then offered a trite response, "But I'll support whatever choice you make."

It didn't take long to decide that my friend and neighbor Brad should be the one to do it. Brad really was one of my best friends. He and his wife, Haywood and I—the four of us were all very close. Plus Brad had been the one who introduced me to the world of abortion moonlighting and helped me make my first connections there. And I trusted Brad.

Haywood and I walked next door to Brad's apartment and sat with him in his beautifully furnished living room.

No thrift-shop, college-student décor here—Brad made a lot of extra money doing abortions, and his wife had excellent taste. "Brad," I said, "I'm four or five weeks pregnant."

"Well, congratulations," he said. "I think. I'm guessing this was unexpected."

"Definitely unexpected," I said. "And I'm not planning to keep it. Will you do an abortion for me?"

Brad's eyes got wide. "Noreen, are you crazy? You and Haywood just got married! And you come asking me to do an abortion for you? Why would you want to kill your baby?"

I was shocked. I'd never heard Brad talk about abortion that way—as killing a baby. "You're the only one I would trust to do it," I said. "I really want you to."

Brad had a funny little chuckle he would give when he was nervous, and he gave that chuckle now. "There's no way I'm doing an abortion for you. It's one thing when I do one as a service for women who come into the clinics. That's just business. I know nothing about their personal lives or their reasons for wanting an abortion, and I don't want to. But this—this would be personal. This would be my good friend's baby. I don't get the reason you don't want to keep it. This baby has everything going for it. You're married. You're both doctors, so money isn't a problem and you can provide whatever this baby needs. No. I won't do it. I love you. I don't want to do anything to harm you."

And he was right that money wasn't the problem. The only problem was that I was selfish and that baby would be inconvenient. I didn't allow my heart to identify with the baby. I hadn't yet developed a mother's heart. For me, it was like a simple problem in logic: I got pregnant unexpectedly,

I'm not willing to make the changes in my life and in my plans that would allow for this baby, so the answer is obvious. I'll have an abortion. Simple logic. Two and two makes four.

But now Brad's refusal was creating a problem in my logical, perfectly ordered, perfectly selfish world. It rattled me. There truly wasn't anyone else I would trust to do it. I couldn't ask Haywood to perform an abortion on his own wife and his own baby, and besides, that would be unethical. Plus, Haywood was on Brad's side! That gave me pause. When I'd told Haywood that I was going to get an abortion, he was initially reserved and careful with his words. After all, it was his baby too.

Only later did I find out that Haywood was waiting to see what my final decision was, and if I decided to go ahead with the abortion, he would talk me out of it. There was no way he was willing to let an abortion happen to our child.

You can see how his attitudes had changed since his college days.

Brad's refusal was a wake-up call for me. Maybe an abortion wasn't the answer after all. Well, at least not for me and Haywood. But I'm sad to confess that I never allowed myself to apply Brad's reasoning to all the babies of the women who came to the abortion facilities where I moonlighted. Never once did I even pause to think about it.

I kept the baby—our daughter Udelle. And who did we ask to be her godfather? Brad.

PART II

New Frontiers

CHAPTER 5

Treading Lightly in the Bible Belt

Noreen

Haywood and I both well remember the day God first revealed to us—or at least to me—that we would be moving from Southern California to, well, someplace else. And the odd thing was, neither of us was walking with the Lord at all at that time of our lives. Haywood, though he'd grown up going to church, had never come to a point of personal faith, and my own spiritual life had been in hibernation for years. We had no relationship with God. But that never means that God does not have a relationship with us. We are His creation! How grateful we are that God doesn't wait for a listening ear before He speaks to a wandering heart.

We were at a party celebrating the end of residency, and all of our fellow residents were there. Haywood was deejaying. He had started out with deejaying modestly, back before I knew him. In fact, to hear him tell it, *modestly* would be an understatement. He had a little cassette player that he could plug a mic into, so that he could turn the music volume down and speak over and between songs—introducing the song or doing typical deejay banter to keep things lively. At first, for parties, he would record everything, song and voiceovers both, on his cassettes—what these days we might call a mixtape. It felt a lot like listening to the radio but with a custom-selected mix of music. Eventually he decided it was more spontaneous and exciting and gave him more flexibility to "work the crowd" if he did the speaking parts live over the prerecorded music.

Great fun! He even had a handle for those mixtapes, and I can still hear it: "This is the Wood, coming to you live from station W-O-O-D …"

Gradually, he worked his way up to some better equipment.

Ask him, and he'll be happy to insist that he used to create some pretty good mixes on those tapes. He knew how to control the mood of the party through the music—to start with easy listening, then bring the mood gradually to a crescendo, ease it back for a breather, then bring it back up.

We could always count on Haywood to create the mood at a party.

The food was great that day—because it had been catered by Mama Robinson, Haywood's mother, and she had made my favorite among her dishes, lasagna. There also would have definitely been some chicken wings, some mac and cheese—and this being a party held by twenty-somethings in LA, there would have been lots of alcohol. Haywood took a break from the mic to come out onto the dance floor and dance with me. I looked around, as we danced, at the others on the dance floor, or sitting around the edges of the room sipping their drinks and talking and laughing and flirting. In LA, a party like this could get pretty wild. Some of the dancers were really dancing! And the voices and laughter were loud.

As always when he deejayed, Haywood was not fully focused on our dancing—I could see that he was preoccupied with what he was going to be doing next with the music. He had pre-recorded the music, of course, but he still had to monitor the mood of the party and get ready to deliver his spoken voiceovers.

He can tell you to this day some of the music he played at that party. He played jazz trumpeter Tom Browne's song "Funkin' for Jamaica" from his *Love Approach* album. Something from Bootsy Collins. All the funk artists.

It struck me with real power, watching and listening to the people at the party, many of them our good friends, that this was not going to be our direction in life. *You don't belong here anymore,* I thought. The music kicked to a higher tempo and got a little louder, and the craziness of the actions around us intensified.

We were engaged but not yet married. We had talked about moving after we married, and had even discussed a specific place to move to and practice medicine: Phoenix, Arizona. But we'd made no decisions. And as I considered our marriage, I thought, *There's no way our marriage will survive this kind of lifestyle. We have to move!*

We danced, I listened, I watched the tipsy, flirting people around me, we danced … and then something hit me. And suddenly it all started unraveling. I stopped dancing. It was as if I was having a vision—a dream in the middle of the dance floor. I waited until the thought became at least somewhat clear in my mind, and then I wanted to share it with him. "Haywood?" I said.

"Hmm?" he said, no doubt wondering why I'd stopped dancing.

"Haywood!" I said.

"What? Are you finished dancing? You hungry?"

"Don't you see it?

Totally confused: "*What?*"

"Don't you see it?"

"See what?"

"We don't belong here." And I could see that so clearly. The lifestyle, the manner of relationships ... Haywood had spent all of his life in Southern California, and I'd been here for years. We'd done our years of residency, met and fallen in love with each other, created strong friendships, and were making great money moonlighting—but despite all that, I could see beyond the shadow of a doubt that while this place would always be part of our past, it was not destined to be part of our future. "We don't belong here, Haywood!"

Still totally confused, Haywood said, "What? What do you mean we don't belong here? Where else would we belong?"

"Haywood," I said, "Don't you—"

"Noreen, I'm trying to deejay the party!"

And I just kept saying, "But don't you see it? Don't you see it?" I felt stunned, the realization was so clear. I had been close to the Lord as a young person, and I grew up with a

72

godly mother, so I knew what I was experiencing. God was speaking to me.

I was seeing all of this in the Spirit. So although I didn't use this language with Haywood, who at that point in his life wouldn't have understood it, what I was saying to myself was, *The Lord is calling us away from this place. He is calling us to a better place, to a land flowing with milk and honey. He will send us to a place where we will thrive, where we will prosper, where the Lord will make our name great, just like Abraham.* I felt as if I were in a trance. It lasted only a moment, and since we were both on the dance floor together, and since the message had been given for us both, I assumed—or hoped, at least—that he was perceiving it along with me.

Did we know that it was Texas we would be called to? No—and I'm sure some will chuckle at the idea of Texas being a "land flowing with milk and honey." All of that would unfold later. But what happened on the dance floor that night, while Haywood's music played, was profound and definite. I knew beyond a doubt that night that we would soon be leaving California.

Interestingly, our dear friend Gail, who I replaced on the Hartford trip where Haywood and I fell on love, said to us about that time, out of the blue, "Why are you thinking about going to Phoenix to practice? Doesn't your brother live in Texas? Why not Texas?"

I thought, *Wow. That sounds like wisdom.*

The time came when we couldn't put off our decision any longer—the end of residency was approaching. We had to decide where we'd be moving. Yes, we could have stayed in LA, making good money working in our medical specialties and performing abortions. But we both knew that the LA lifestyle would threaten and could eventually destroy us—our future as a couple, our marriage, and our business plans. LA was a place where Haywood had had, shall we say, way too much fun. Besides our own vulnerabilities, we were seeing some well-respected and prosperous physicians lose everything they had worked hard for because of poor lifestyle choices. We weren't willing to take that risk. We had to move. But where?

My brother Royce, a family physician in Austin, Texas, invited Haywood to visit. While Haywood was there, one of my brother's friends suggested he look at the twin cities of Bryan/College Station. "You'd be filling a real need," he said. "I think there's only one Black physician in the area. Plus, they're creating a new medical school at Texas A&M University, right there in Bryan. If you want to teach, I'm sure they'll give you an interview if they hear you're moving there."

Now Gail's suggestion was starting to make a lot of sense.

So a day or two later, I got a phone call from Haywood, who was so excited he could barely get his words out. "I found it!" he said. "Our new home!" When he told me the name of the place, I pulled out an atlas and scanned the huge state of Texas—I couldn't even find Bryan or College Station! But one thing I did recognize: The enthusiasm I was hearing in Haywood's voice was the same excitement I had felt when, out on the dance floor that night, I received the vision of the land flowing with milk and honey.

"And not only would we be the only Black doctors in that particular market, but better yet, we would be the only abortionists! We would make a killing!"

The macabre pun was, I'm sure, unintentional, because at the time we didn't think of abortion as killing.

And that's how, on October 3 of 1981, we arrived in Bryan/College Station in a yellow Toyota Celica towing a yellow Volkswagen Beetle. I was twelve weeks pregnant with Udelle. The baby I had planned to abort.

Haywood

That was the last time I drove a major part of I-10, and I don't ever want to do it again. Mile after mile of mostly flat, mostly hot, mostly desert land. Growing up in Southern California, with the ocean to the west and snow-covered mountains to the north and east, both of them within just a couple hours' drive, I was used to landscapes with a bit more variety.

We were fortunate that Royce, Noreen's brother, like us a doctor, lived nearby. He's a genius at details and logistics, and he helped us deal with the many nuances of how you set up a practice—getting licensed in Texas and a long list of other things. With his help, we were able to get it all done and begin seeing patients within a short three or four weeks.

We discovered that there was no space available for lease in Bryan/College Station that was suitable for a medical office, at least not without major renovations. We did, though, find two brothers, both doctors, who had their practice there. They had been the first doctors in Bryan/College Station to desegregate their reception room, way back in the late '50s—just a reminder that we were now living and working in the South.

One of the brothers, James—Dr. James F. Cooper (he went by JF)—said, "Noreen and Haywood, why don't you locate your practice here, in my office? I have exam rooms you can use to get started." We felt so fortunate—this man we barely knew was throwing his arms open to us and welcoming us into his own space until we could find our own.

He was an icon in the Bryan/College Station medical world, and even beyond. He believed in doing things on the basis of right and wrong, not on the basis of how much money it was going to make him and whether it would keep him in the country club.

We started practicing there in November of '81. We found another space that we thought would work for us long term, only a few blocks from JF's space, but it needed improvements and remodeling, so we stayed with JF till April of '82, then moved into our own space.

Being able to share office space with JF was a big deal for us, because it meant we would have income for the five months it would take us to remodel the office space we had chosen to purchase.

We were treated wonderfully in that town. When we found the space we wanted for our medical office, a banker by the name of Churchill Jones loaned us enough for the down payment—and then approved a mortgage for us for the balance. How often are you able to buy any kind of commercial space under those arrangements, with no money to your name? His bank saw promise in us, and they were willing to take a chance, and we were thankful for it. We found favor. I didn't know the Lord at that time, but now I would describe it as prevenient grace—God working behind the scenes, even before conversion, to get us to where He had planned for us to be.

Udelle was born in April of '82. Our precious honeymoon baby. How grateful we were now to Brad for being a champion for her life. We wanted to be a regular American family, and we thought that meant we should attend church. After all, Noreen and I had both grown up attending church. We visited two or three traditional, liturgical churches, gave each of them what we considered to be a fair shot, but each time we could see this just wasn't for us.

Visiting the kind of church I grew up in reminded me of why the teenaged version of me had lost interest in attending them back then. So much sameness. At 10:45, the organ strikes up. Choir walks in. Everything is done the same way every week. About the time the choir launches into one of the same four or five songs they always sing (or so it felt to me), I slip into daydream mode and I'm lost for the rest of the service.

After we moved to Texas, I missed my deejaying so much I came back to it a couple of years later, about 1983. I got a gig at a local radio station doing a three-hour Saturday morning show. I kept the same handle: "This is the Wood, coming to you live from the House of Incense and Peppermint and strange little happenings, mixing and blending a little musical brew just for you ..." I played anything from mainstream jazz to R&B. And that's how I spent my Saturday mornings for a few years. But not alone. My twin brother Howard would come to the station and assist me. That turned out to be a meaningful way for us to connect at a level we hadn't since our high school days. And I loved being a voice on the airwaves to our new community.

Of course, I had no inkling that a time would come when God would use that voice of mine to speak His truth in that same community.

CHAPTER 6

Abortion on the Down-Low

Haywood

In Bryan/College Station, we incorporated as Brazos Medical Associates (since we were in Brazos County). I did family practice and Noreen did OBGYN. We both delivered babies.

When we started practice, I remember being amazed every day at how small the area was, in comparison to LA. I would get into my car in the morning—the little yellow VW. I always played music when I drove, so I would push the cassette in, a song would start, and I would drive out of the condominium parking lot and pass one stop sign, then another, then another. Three stop signs, and then I was at our office. And the same song that had started playing when I pulled out of the condominium complex was still playing when I pulled into our parking lot. Surreal! Back in LA, I would usually have played two whole cassette tapes on my commute. Here—less than one song.

When Udelle was born, Noreen could go home from our office, breastfeed her, then come back and see her afternoon patients. How refreshing and strange to live in an area where everything was within a fifteen- or twenty-minute drive.

That wasn't the only unusual thing we found in Texas, though. We found that we had to adjust to some attitudes that were far different from those we were used to in Southern California. One funny example happened after one of the flights we'd taken to Texas to scope out the area. It was actually Noreen's first trip to Austin. Neither of us had spent much time in Texas, and although Noreen had lived in Trinidad and DC, I had lived only in Southern California. So neither of us had any experience with Texas culture or attitudes.

At the time, Noreen had braids with beads on them—very stylish in 1980.

We landed at the Austin airport and proceeded down to baggage claim. And suddenly there's a good ol' boy, complete with western hat and boots, shirt with snaps instead of buttons, and he's standing next to us staring at Noreen. We had never seen him before. He reaches out and takes hold of Noreen's beaded and braided hair as if he has some right to examine it! And he says, "What're those gizmos in your hair?"

Noreen, at a complete loss for what to do, looks at me and says, "Gizmos?"

Stating the obvious, I just say, "Well—those are beads."

Talk about culture shock! In Southern California, no

one would have simply reached out without permission and touched a stranger's hair. It would have been considered unacceptably intimate and rude.

Welcome to Texas!

Maybe that was a lost job opportunity! We could have opened a gizmo shop.

Noreen

Besides my regular OBGYN appointments, I was also doing abortions. But only on the down-low.

That's because of some excellent advice we were given very early in our time in Bryan/College Station. As is customary, new physicians in a community visit the offices of their physician colleagues to introduce themselves. When we met for the first time with Dr. Robert Benbow, a gray-haired elder statesman of the Bryan/College Station medical community, the oldest OBGYN in town, he asked bluntly, "Are you planning to perform abortions?"

I said, "Yes. There's nobody else in town doing them."

"Well, young lady," he said, "if I were you, I'd tread very, very lightly on those grounds. This is still the Bible belt. And you don't want to be known as the town abortionist."

I was shocked. I had actually been feeling genuinely proud to be making abortions available in this area where they previously had not been. I'd really considered it a missing service here, and I was proud to fill that gap. Haywood was with me that day, and he was just as surprised. But when you get a word of advice from an older sage, you'd better listen. You want to respect his years of experience and wisdom.

He was giving good sound advice, and I listened carefully. "Tread lightly on those grounds," he'd said. I didn't take that to mean not to offer abortions at all, but rather to evaluate very carefully just *who* I did abortions on. And how public I should be about it.

So when I began offering abortions, I did so only clandestinely on select patients whom I thought I could trust with our little secret. And I thought that approach must be working, because no one said anything to me about it. *If any of the other doctors are aware of it,* I thought, *they must have decided it's best ignored.*

My brother Royce in Austin had asked whether we might want to teach in a medical school. We did, actually, and that being true, we moved to Bryan/College Station at just the right time. The big university—the "college" in College Station—is Texas A&M. They had begun a medical school, Texas A&M College of Medicine, just a few years before, and the first graduating class was the year Haywood and I moved to Bryan/College Station, 1981. We began teaching there almost immediately, eventually finding ourselves on the admissions committee.

I may not have performed abortions on many women during that period in Bryan/College Station, but two of them were women who were very close to me. The first was Amy. She was married to Jim, who was working on his graduate degree at the time. Their first child was healthy. However, their second child had birth defects that were incompatible with life and did not survive. They brought their third child to Haywood for a routine well-infant check. It was at that time we all developed a friendship and became close.

Amy had an unexpected pregnancy with their fourth child that she did not welcome. Amy said, "I don't want this baby. My husband is in grad school. I'm high risk anyway—I've already lost one baby. And I'm older now, so I'm at even higher risk for genetic complications to occur. Noreen—" She was near tears now. "You would be doing me a favor. And this baby too."

Amy was one of my best friends. I'd have preferred to not do the abortion—but at the same time, I truly did, at that point in my life, believe that abortion was an acceptable tool in situations like this. As Amy had said, there was a possible health risk for this baby, but the truth is, I aborted what was most likely a healthy baby.

And Amy wasn't the only woman close to me on whom I performed an abortion during that short period—I'll write about the other one, even closer to me, in a later chapter.

Then one day, a patient I didn't know showed up at the office asking for an abortion. I was a little suspicious, so I said, "Abortions aren't available in this town. Why did you come to me for one?"

Looking confused, she said, "I was referred by my primary care doctor—Dr. Rastogi."

Dr. Rastogi and I had never discussed my willingness to do abortions. Yet somehow, he had found out. And if he knew, then others knew. So it was no longer a secret. I had indeed become the town abortionist. Now my reputation was on the line.

I was sad to give it up, though, for two reasons. For one, I did still think of it as an important service that should be available to any woman, regardless of what part of the country she lived in. And the second reason was, I confess, the money. Truthfully, I wasn't charging much, or sometimes anything at all, for the procedure. We were no longer in the position we'd been in as residents in LA, when we would scrimp if we didn't do abortions, or have more money than we needed if we did them. Now our income was comfortable, whether we were performing abortions or not.

Our only employee at the time was an LVN (licensed vocational nurse) and office manager rolled into one, a Catholic woman. She said, "Dr. Johnson, if you're going to be doing this kind of dirty work, you'd better start charging people for it."

And eventually I would have. But for now, I saw it as worth doing even for free because I really felt I was helping the community. You see how persuasive the enemy can be? I was now the benevolent doctor because I was doing abortions. The community had been deprived of a service—now I was providing that service. So, in my mind, it wasn't about the money then, even though that's exactly why Haywood and I had done abortions in California. I thought if the demand for abortions continued to grow and I was the only one doing them, then of course I would have more patients—and the money would come. But at the time, the devil had me convinced I was doing the right thing—helping out women who needed an alternative.

I saw, at that stage of my life, no problem with the procedure itself. But I wanted to practice mainstream medicine, and I began to fear that continuing to offer abortions might cause me to be seen, as Dr. Benbow had intimated, as a back-alley quack. I wanted to be respected among my peers and in the community, so I resigned myself to discontinue performing abortions.

PART III

The Awakening

CHAPTER 7

The Concert

Haywood

"I think you might like this, Haywood," said a patient of mine, Terry Teykl, as he handed me a cassette tape at the end of an office visit.

There are moments in life—seemingly ordinary moments—that set into motion great life-changing turning points. This was one of those moments. But of course, I had no idea of that at the time. I thought a friendly patient who knew I loved music was simply being kind. I was clueless that my entire life, my eternity in fact, was about to change. You've got to love how God works!

"Thanks, Terry. Leon Patillo? Haven't heard of him."

"He used to play keyboards and sing with the rock band Santana."

Truth is, Terry was more than just a patient. He was my mom's neighbor. Shortly after Mama moved to College

Station to help us care for Udelle, his wife, Kay, became one of my patients (probably because Mama recommended me), and Terry followed not long after.

Terry was the founding pastor of Aldersgate Church. I have to say, God really broke the mold after he made Terry. He was known as the motorcycle-riding preacher, for reasons that quickly became obvious once you knew him. A very bright guy with an immense passion for souls. So, when my mother moved into his neighborhood, and eventually my brother too, Terry and Kay reached out.

Terry was right. I really did like the tape. It quickly became one of my favorites. At this point I wasn't attending church—Terry's or anyone else's. I wasn't even saved, much less into Christian music. But I didn't think of it as a Christian album at all—I just thought it was great music.

Several weeks later Terry invited Noreen and me to lunch. The restaurant we chose was Fish Richards, in an old house on Wellborn Road that has since been torn down. It was a fine-dining-type place with excellent gourmet seafood. Noreen and I both loved good seafood, and when we first arrived in College Station, we asked someone what good seafood restaurants he could recommend. He thought it over, nodded, and said, "Well—we have Long John Silver."

There was a pause, and then Noreen managed to say "Thank you" without laughing, but we both had a good laugh about it later. Don't get me wrong—I'm sure Long John Silver has its place, especially for someone looking for an alternative to a fast-food hamburger. But when Noreen and I said *seafood*, we were talking about the lick your lips, congratulate the chef kind of super-fresh seafood that in those days was available only fairly close to the ocean and that you recall fondly for days afterward. And Fish Richards was that kind of place.

You know how you can tell somebody really feels they have to say something, by the way they're restless and fidgety? During that lunch, Terry was like that. Finally he came out with it: "Haywood, I've got to tell you something. The Lord told me to tell you that you're going to be a strong Christian leader in this town." And once he'd gotten that off his chest, he sat back and relaxed.

He could relax. But I was confused. A strong Christian leader? I didn't know what to make of that. But it wouldn't be in character for me to freak out about something like that. Haywood had to always look smooth, always be cool. I wasn't going to look shook up, right? Was I startled? You bet. But one thing you learn as a doctor is how to not show the emotion you're really feeling. You can't gasp and say, "You mean you've had *seven* abortions? *Seven?*" No. You remain calm and say, "Seven abortions. Can you tell me about when each of them took place, and the circumstances?" Just the facts, ma'am.

So when Terry said what he said about me as a Christian leader, I was thinking, *Who the heck*—only at that point in my life, I didn't say *heck—who the heck is he, coming to me, telling me what I'm going to do?* You can hear my worldly thinking, can't you? Because in the world, you don't want anybody telling you what you're going to do. *I* decide what I'm going to do. *I* make the decisions. Haywood is lord. Like most believers, before I submitted to the Lordship of Jesus Christ, that's how I thought. Christian leader, he says?

Well, maybe someday I would visit his church, but that's it. Christian leader? Not likely.

That's what was rumbling inside me as we sat there at lunch. But I was smiling. I probably had a beer—and some incredible seafood. I was very cordial. I wasn't angry—but I sure thought he was out of line. Who was he to be telling me this?

As we walked to our car in the parking lot after lunch, I turned to Noreen and said something like, "What's with that guy? Is he crazy? Was he really telling me what I'm going to do with my life?"

Noreen shrugged it off: "He's a little bit different. A little weird."

I didn't make any connection between what he'd said at lunch and the cassette tape he'd given me. Leon's album was just good, solid music to me. I would sing along with it—loud!—"*J-E-S-U-S! J-E-S-U-S! He's my superstar!*" But I wasn't processing it as spiritual content. I was just processing it as music that I enjoyed.

I was still doing some deejaying, and at the radio station one day I saw a concert poster announcing—guess what—a Leon Patillo concert ... in College Station. And what was the venue? Aldersgate Church—Terry Teykl's church! Where he pastored. And I said, "Huh. Leon Patillo's coming to town. How come that pastor, who gave me the Leon Patillo cassette in the first place, didn't get back to me and tell me Leon's coming?" I wasn't angry. But I was disappointed that he hadn't thought about me. I was his doctor, for pete's sake! A very important person! He could have brought some tickets to my office!

And I really did want to go hear Leon. So I bought my own tickets, two of them. Most of the time, heading to a concert, Noreen would have been right there with me. But she was about thirty-six weeks pregnant with our second child and had no desire to sit through a concert, even though by that time she was very familiar with Leon's music, because that cassette had become the main music I played in my car. She just wanted to stay home and put her feet up to keep the swelling down.

All this happened on a Sunday night, March 2, 1986—a mild, clear day. I climbed into my Volkswagen. I loved that car. I hadn't customized it much, but I did have some great-looking mag rims. And back in those days, even in California where I'd bought it, a lot of cars didn't have air conditioning. We had what we called two-sixty air conditioning. Two windows down at sixty miles an hour. Such a simple car to maintain. No oil filter. It had an oil screen. It had four sparkplugs. Little bitty motor. But such a fun car to drive.

So I picked up my mother who lived about two miles away. She knew Terry and his wife well and was looking forward to seeing Terry's church.

We went in, my mama and I, and found our seats. (Today, almost every time I go to church—still my home church these many years later—I look over, as close as I can remember, to the spot where we sat that day.) As I picture the two of us side by side in church, I can't help but think back to my days as a child, sitting next to her in our church every Sunday.

Mama took Howard and me to church from the very beginning. We were both baptized in the CME church—which originally meant *Colored* Methodist Episcopal but was eventually changed to Christian Methodist Episcopal. Either way, it's a Methodist denomination for Blacks, just like the AME—African Methodist Episcopal. The Methodist denomination of the time wouldn't ordain Blacks, so Blacks started the AME and CME churches. I attended all the way through high school.

My twin brother Howard and I, like brothers everywhere, would squabble if we sat together, so Mama sat between us. Howard, who didn't really like being around people as much as I did, would sit on the aisle—right *on* the aisle, every week. Mama would be in the next seat, and I always sat next to Mama. (My father didn't go to church as I was growing up. He never, to my knowledge, got saved.) And when the offering plate came by, Mama would give us each seven cents for the benevolent offering—there were always *two* offerings— and ten cents for the regular offering.

The services were liturgical. However, in Black culture there is commonly a lively air to the service, and many times people, especially women, would "get happy"—shouting, passing out, etc.

And you'd always get a program in church, typed and mimeographed in those days. On the backside they listed the people who were sick and shut-in. And Mama and Aunt Mildred, her sister, used to always take the program home—

in fact, they saved every program until there was a tall stack of them.

Every Sunday morning, at exactly 10:45, Eunice Blackwell would start playing that Hammond organ. The choir would walk up the aisles from the back. They would proceed into the choir loft and sing a few songs. The same thing every Sunday for seventeen years. And I would just zone out until it was over and we would go home. On occasion we would go to Aunt Mildred's home after church, only about four blocks from the church.

It sounds funny now, but there was a big, blue neon sign on top of that church that said, "Jesus Saves." You could see it from blocks away. As long as I went to that church, I never knew what that meant: Jesus Saves. You would think that, at some point, someone would have explained it. Or maybe someone did but I didn't have ears to hear.

Small wonder, then, that when I headed off to college, I didn't attend church. When I got to medical school, I discovered my roommate Calvin was the son of a Pentecostal preacher—who, interestingly enough, was one of the people who had interviewed me for admission into medical school.

The concert began, and we were both really enjoying it. My mother liked music, too—in fact, one thing I remember from growing up is that she could really, really dance. The jitterbug and all that.

Then in the middle of the concert, something happened. And when I say something, I really mean *something*.

Something huge and unexpected. But the funny thing was, it didn't seem like much at the time. It was just so simple. Leon was talking between songs, and he didn't say, "Jesus died on the cross for your sins." He didn't say, "His blood saved you." I don't even remember him mentioning sin. He didn't trot out the four spiritual laws. But God knew what I needed to hear, what I would respond to. If Leon had tried to challenge me about my sins, I'd have had a problem with that—because remember, Haywood was lord of his own life. But Leon just said, "Anybody who wants things to be 100 percent right with God—just stand up right now."

Who could turn that down? Yeah, I'll take 100 percent. Sure, I'm standing up for that. I have to say—I really didn't understand all that my standing up would mean, what Jesus' death on the cross really had to do with it. If I had, I probably would have kept my seat and thought it over good before I got up. But the Holy Spirit (even though I didn't know it was the Holy Spirit then) yanked me up so fast!

So now I'm standing. But once I was on my feet, I was really kind of wishing I could sit back down—but that, I thought, would probably draw even more attention. So I was trying to stay completely motionless so no one would notice me.

And then while we were still standing, me and the rest scattered around the auditorium, Leon prayed. I don't remember exactly what he prayed. It was very short. And in the end he just said, "Amen," and started the music again.

I sat back down. What did I think? I didn't know. I might have thought now maybe things would get a little bit better in my life. I wasn't sure, because I didn't really understand what my standing up to get things 100 percent right with God meant.

What was Mama doing all that time, seated right beside me? Knowing her, she must have been praying. But I actually never asked her.

The concert ended. The lights came up. Leon had done a great job. And to my surprise, a few people came up to me with great excitement. One of them, whom I later found out was Nancy Coen, a real fixture in the church, congratulated me on choosing to follow God by standing. I didn't know why she was so excited. I just wanted things to be right with God. I didn't really grasp what she and the others were congratulating me about.

Sitting near me in the crowd was somebody who worked in the bank I used. Later, she told me that she saw me stand and accept the Lord. But if you had asked me at the end of that concert if I had "accepted the Lord" by standing, I'd have wondered what you were talking about.

When I got home from the concert, I had the first glimpse of how much things had changed for me without my even knowing it. I opened the refrigerator. I always had a six-pack of Heineken there. And this time, I had a surreal experience. You know that special effects thing they do in the movies—where you focus on something but suddenly it moves way, way, way, *way* back? Well, it suddenly looked like that refrigerator was ten feet deep and that six-pack of Heineken was clear at the back of it, far away from me. *Strange,* I thought. *Why does it look like that?* So I didn't pull a beer out, even though that's what I'd opened the refrigerator to do. I wasn't doing it to prove anything to anybody—in fact, there wasn't anybody there. Noreen was resting in the back of the house. I was by myself.

I shut the refrigerator door, perplexed. *Is this connected to this 100-percent-right-with-God thing?* I wondered. *What's this strange feeling?* The best way John Wesley could describe his Aldersgate Street conversion in England long ago was as a "heartwarming experience." I wouldn't necessarily say *heartwarming*. I would describe my feelings that night as *strangely perplexing*. The whole depth-perception illusion with the refrigerator was just ... weird. Something was definitely different. It was as if I'd managed to get the first three pieces of a five-hundred-piece puzzle put together.

Within a couple of weeks, a few more pieces of the puzzle came together when I started getting up at 6:30 a.m. to go meet with a few other men, only six or seven of us, for a weekly prayer time. Getting up at 6:30? To go pray? Believe me, I'd never done anything like that before. The only praying I'd done was as a kid, saying the Lord's Prayer just before crawling into bed. Talking to God was as alien to me as talking to ... well, aliens.

At these morning prayer sessions, the men around me were praying things like, "Oh, Lord, do this for Brother Jones. Please heal Sister Brown." All of that was completely foreign to me. Christian TV was in its infancy then, and I never watched it anyway. I think I might have watched one night of a Billy Graham crusade on TV, with George Beverly Shea singing and Cliff Barrow leading the choir and throngs of people coming down to receive Christ. I didn't know what those people were walking down to the front for. But I knew who Billy Graham was. In fact, Mama was living in LA when

Billy Graham got his start there. She actually went to see Billy Graham.

So I'd never had an experience with prayer where I actually felt like I was talking to someone. Meeting with those men in those early mornings, for the first time I could feel that there was something going on. A connection. A real connection with this God that I previously had known nothing about. Later, I would learn about the role the Holy Spirit played in that, but at the time I knew nothing about the Holy Spirit—knew nothing, in fact, about the Bible. The Bible is full of examples of prayer. I was fascinated, listening to those men pray. In every one of those prayer meetings, something new would be revealed. As they prayed out loud, the men would say things like, "Lord, you say in your Word ..." and they would mention a chapter and verse. *How did they know that chapter and verse?* I didn't even know what the numbers meant after the name of a book of the Bible—two numbers divided by a colon—what did that mean? And if somebody said, "Go to Jeremiah," I would have to go to the table of contents and find the page number.

It was like being thrown into the deep end of the pool when previously all I'd been exposed to was a glass of water. And I began to grasp the truth: This thing—Christianity— was actually real and alive. Alive! Not just some kind of mental or social exercise. And it was changing me. I was actually eager to come back the next day and see what else I could learn. Having been an athlete as a younger man, I'd learned the importance of training. This was kind of like that. *Let me go to the gym! Let me get together with my training partners!*

Let me hear more from these guys, or from the person who leads praise and worship.

Two weeks after the concert, Calvin came to visit, along with his wife, Sarajane. We had asked him to be the godfather of our newborn, Riva. Thinking maybe he could help me make sense of the whole thing, I told him about the concert, about standing up when Leon invited me to, even about the refrigerator experience. It was the first time I'd told anyone about any of that. And when I got that far, Calvin started to cry.

"Haywood," he said, "Sarajane and I have been praying for you and Noreen to come to Christ."

I wasn't sure what he meant by that, so he went on to explain. And I can't say that all the puzzle pieces fell into place that night, but a few did. As he spoke, I kept thinking, *Okay, I'm starting to get it.*

Here's a strange thing. Even though, by the time Calvin and his wife came to visit, it had been at least a couple of weeks since the Leon Patillo concert, *I had said nothing to Noreen about it at all!* As I was telling Calvin about it, Noreen was hearing it all for the first time. Why hadn't I told her? I had probably used her pregnancy as an excuse—thinking something like, *When a woman is this pregnant, well over thirty weeks, you don't want to upset her by describing strange experiences you don't understand yourself.* So the night of the concert I probably just said something like, "Honey, I'm home. Wow—that was a great concert. Man! Just like I expected, Leon Patillo was really good." Based on my limited understanding at the time, what could I have said? "Honey, I had a weird experience with the refrigerator just now and

I feel funny." I'd have expected her to say something like, "What do you need? Tylenol? Pepto-Bismol?"

But after the conversation with Calvin, the cat was out of the bag. And as it turned out, Noreen had not been unaware that I'd been going through some changes, which I'll let her describe in the next chapter.

Noreen and I talked it over after Calvin and his wife left and decided that we should start to attend church. But which one?

CHAPTER 8

Reawakening

Noreen

Growing up in Trinidad, I was the last of six children. Four brothers came first, but my dad still wanted a daughter, and at last they got one—my sister Arlene.

They spoiled her, of course—especially my dad. She was his pride and joy. But he was also very strict with her, very protective. Of me as well. Neither of us, for instance, was allowed to ride a bike. My brothers could ride bikes, but in my father's eyes, it wasn't proper for a girl to sit with her legs straddling a bicycle. And this wasn't because of religious conviction—my father was by no means a religious man. He'd been raised Anglican, but he was not a churchgoer. My mom, on the other hand, was Baptist and went to church at every opportunity. She was a praying woman, a serious woman of God. Since the age of fourteen, she never wavered or backslid. She lived to be one hundred and three years old.

My father was a very good provider. He was a forest conservator, or what we know today as a forest ranger. We had a big house, so many people we knew considered us wealthy, but of course we weren't. It's just that my mother was very frugal. My father turned his paycheck over to her, and she managed the money well.

In fact, my brothers joked about how she would sew all their clothes, even their pants. They cheered and laughed when they finally got pants that had a fob—that little extra pocket on the front, a fifth pocket, for change or a watch. My brothers wore shorts all the time until they were in their mid-teens or later, but that wasn't from frugality or strictness—that was just the custom in Trinidad. Long pants were a rite of passage to manhood. A family that sent its teenaged boys out in public with long pants would be sending a message of being too uppity. It would be disrespectful.

Our house had two stories—unusual in our area. But we needed the space. We had six children, and in addition, we were always taking people in. Both of my parents were generous and hospitable. We always had plenty, enough to share. In those days, families helped other families. They didn't have government welfare to rely on. Over the years, we took in three other boys for long periods of time, boys from families my parents had known in the part of Trinidad along the remote north coast, where they had lived before I was born.

So my memories of growing up include my four brothers, but also three other young men my brothers' age. All of the boys slept downstairs. Arlene and I slept upstairs, where Momma and Daddy slept.

It was a wonderful house—and still is. Its teak floors and

doors have held up beautifully since it was built in the '50s. Everyone else has either passed away or moved away, but my sister Arlene lives there still.

We lived in San Fernando, the most populous city in Trinidad (Port of Spain is the capitol.) San Fernando is where the island's oil is, and that's why it's considered to be the industrial capitol. The oil refinery was located in the area where I grew up.

When Arlene was seventeen or eighteen, she got pregnant. Nobody in my family knew. She had an abortion. That was a typical way of dealing with such problems even back in the day, and sometimes that meant the proverbial back-alley abortions. But in my sister's case, the abortion was done by a doctor. It was illegal, of course. But my aunt—well, we called her aunt, but she was actually my mother's first cousin—was friends with a lot of the doctors at the hospital. She arranged for one of them to give Arlene an abortion. Weeks later, somehow word of the pregnancy and abortion leaked out.

Arlene and I were very close growing up, even though she was four years older. Like sisters everywhere, one minute we'd be fighting, the next minute hugging and kissing. We were so close, and yet while she was going through all of this, I never knew. I never knew. I would have been thirteen or fourteen. She was still living at home.

When my parents found out, my dad hit the roof. He blamed my mom, because he believed she hadn't been watching us closely enough. "If you had been," he yelled, "how could she have spent time alone with a boyfriend—much less gotten pregnant?" Why hadn't my father been home to watch over her himself? Because, as a park ranger, he needed to travel. He would leave on Mondays and come home on Fridays, camping away from home in the countryside, watching over the government's forests while my mom was supposed to be watching over his girls every hour of the day.

After her abortion, Arlene was unclean in my father's eyes, and couldn't be redeemed. Now his attention turned to me. "I'm going to have to separate Arlene and you," he said.

"What? No!" I said. "We've never been separated! She's not just my sister, she's my best friend!"

"She's made her choice," he said, "and it's for a way of life that will contaminate you if I don't protect you from it."

Once my father had said it, I knew it would happen. There was no appeal from his decisions. But how would it happen? Would they send Arlene away? Me?

Sometimes I can't even think about those days, or speak about them, without tears coming to my eyes. They sent me to live with my oldest brother, Frank, thirteen years older than me. He had gotten married. So I was still living with a brother, with family, but separated now from the house I had always known, from my mom, my sister (who was now unclean), my other brothers, my neighborhood friends.

There were hidden blessings, of course. There always are. Frank, more than anyone else, influenced me spiritually. I would have to say that he's the one responsible for my salvation.

That's when my father really began to persecute my mom. He truly did blame her, even more than Arlene, for Arlene's pregnancy and abortion. When I would come home, I would find my mom nearly catatonic. Her response to my father's extreme persecution was to stop talking. My mom was a godly and spiritual woman throughout her life, but during this period, she withdrew into herself. Even when I was in the room with her, she would just sit and stare. Maybe she had cried so much that she had exhausted all the tears. She would look at me, but with no expression.

I lived with Frank for about a year. After that, maybe my father realized that it wasn't good for me to be separated from most of my family, and he allowed me to come back home. Arlene and I rekindled our relationship, and we were always fine with each other after that. I knew she'd had the abortion. She told me about it. And after she'd told me, we never talked about it again.

I was in high school by that time. My parents, my father in particular, seemed to by then have become a little more liberal in how they raised us. I even started driving. I did all of the normal stuff teenagers do.

Having seen the effect of Arlene's choices on my family, especially on my parents, I swore I would be Miss Goody-Goody Two-Shoes. I wouldn't make the mistakes Arlene had made. I wouldn't hurt my parents.

I started driving Momma to her Baptist church. Her church was about a half-hour's drive from our home. I connected with the wonderful youth group there. I made friends among them, and spent a great deal of time with those teenagers. Although that period didn't last a long time, it had a lasting effect. I was very active in church life then.

Arlene became a teacher shortly after that and left home to attend teacher's college.

Our family structure may seem odd to those unfamiliar with customs in Trinidad. My sister Arlene and I, the two youngest siblings, were paired up with two of our older brothers who then bore some responsibility for us. I was paired up with my brother Glen, the physician, the one in whose footsteps I would follow. We call him by his middle name, Royce. I remember two momentous occasions on which he left home. The first time was to teach at Presentation College, one of the most prestigious colleges in Trinidad. Understand that when I say college, that's what Americans would call high school—in Trinidad, we used the terms often used in the British educational system. And there is some overlap—if you're a top student in Trinidad, then by the time you graduate from what Americans would call high school and have taken your A-level exams, you have actually finished the equivalent of your first two years of undergraduate study.

Understand, too, that when I say it was a fond memory, that wasn't because he was leaving home. It was because we were all so proud of him for winning this important job.

He taught there for about two years before he went off to Howard University in the United States, the second time he left home. And after graduation from Howard, on to medical school and family residency.

In those days, not many young people left the islands to study. Most went to Jamaica to study at the University of the West Indies. The Jamaica campus was the only one at the time; there wasn't a Trinidad campus until I reached college age myself. Now they have campuses on most of the larger islands. Trinidadians who didn't want to attend the University of the West Indies went to the UK to study. Very few came to the US. My brother was among those few.

Going to the airport to leave Trinidad was a big event. If somebody in your family was going away to study, especially to study medicine, all the family would go to the airport to wave goodbye. And in those days you could get as close to your loved one as you wanted for as long as you wanted, right up until time for the plane to take off.

The custom was, if you were traveling, you were well dressed. None of this traveling in shorts and a T-shirt and flip-flops! You left home in a suit. So my brother wore a suit and tie, and the rest of us were dressed up to see him off. And I wanted to carry his briefcase. So as we were walking into the airport, my brother walked first and I walked behind him, carrying his briefcase. Literally, I was following in his footsteps—because this was *my* brother, Royce, the one with whom I had been paired. He was going to the US to study medicine. In only a few more years, I would follow in his footsteps once again and move to the US to attend first Howard University and then the Howard University College of Medicine.

At the time Royce left for the US, though, I wasn't thinking about a career in medicine. I wanted to be a chemist. It wasn't until about my second year of high school that I started dissecting animals and found that I *loved* the dissection process, *loved* exploring the body, taking it apart. As my sister Arlene loves to recall, I did the first heart transplant on a frog.

In my school, we had to catch our own frogs for dissection—and we had giant frogs (actually toads) in Trinidad, called cane toads or *crapaud*. I was the lab assistant, a prestigious position to have. It even paid about ten dollars a week, big money back then. As lab assistant, I had access to chloroform, which I could use to anesthetize the frogs. So one day I anesthetized a frog, took its heart out, and put it back in and reconnected it. To my surprise, it went right on beating, prompting Arlene's teasing about "the first successful heart transplant."

And although that little exercise was no different from the kinds of exercises students perform in every biology or physiology course around the world, it was for me a precursor of what was to come. I was truly fascinated by the body, and the function of the internal organs. I love to take it apart and put it back together, just the way it was before but with whatever was wrong with it fixed. To me, that's a miracle.

My mom was, as I've said, a godly woman, a woman of prayer. And she needed to be, given the challenges she faced in life. She lived to be over a hundred, and part of her motivation in striving to live so long, to keep up her health, to remain active even long after most people have died, was that she felt she had to take care of one my brothers, Carl. He had cerebral palsy. Throughout his life, he progressively got worse. He could still walk after he'd reached adulthood, but with the characteristic ataxic gait of the cerebral palsy patient. Eventually, though, he had to be in a wheelchair, and then bedridden. Clearly, his life was hard. I once heard him pray, "Why me, Lord?"

Because of her commitment to taking care of Carl, Momma remained functional past the age of one hundred.

Believe it or not, even at ninety years old, she was actually cutting coconuts with a machete out in the yard. We even caught her trying to climb the avocado tree.

Seeing my mom praying on her knees on those hard teak floors is one of my earliest memories, and she continued that well into her nineties. She would kneel by her bed, steadying herself with a hand on the bedclothes. I've never seen anyone so motionless. And there was a system to her prayer. I would hear her walking through the family tree, praying for every child and grandchild by name. In the morning, and again at night. Praying for and interceding for her family.

My father, in contrast, made sure we were confirmed in the Anglican church, because that was the faith tradition he was brought up in. But he never went to church himself. He sent us and made sure we attended. But after the massive disruption of our family relationships after Arlene's pregnancy and abortion and I was sent to live with my brother Frank, my father was unable to affect my church attendance one way or another. It was an incredibly hard time for all of us, and I missed my mom, missed my home, missed my best friend and sister Arlene. I was hungry for reassurance and stability, so even though my father was no longer there to insist on my attending church, my brother Frank gently encouraged me to go with him to his church on Sundays. When he had left home, he had gravitated away from the Anglican church and begun attending a Pentecostal church. That's the church I attended with Frank, and that's where I accepted Jesus. I was probably thirteen.

After that, I was eager to learn more about the Lord. I

started going to Sunday school at Frank's church. But that spiritual hunger didn't last long.

Once I was out of high school, I did my first year of university in Trinidad at the University of the West Indies. Other than the year I spent living with Frank, that was my first year of *freedom*, away from what I considered to be my father's strictness. To be fair, by then he was a little more mellow. But he was still strict enough that, living at home, I had been held in check. Not that I had any desire to be wild and crazy. Even at the University of the West Indies, where I stayed in a dorm, I didn't act out much.

When I came to the US, to Washington, DC, after my one year of college in Trinidad, my favorite brother, Royce, was already a physician, married and with his first child. In good Trinidadian custom, I lived with him throughout undergraduate school and medical school, and that saved a lot of money.

My father paid most of my expenses as an undergraduate and in medical school at Howard. Thank God I was bright enough to get scholarships to cover whatever expenses he didn't cover. I would have been happy to get a job to earn part of the cost, but my father said, "No, I don't want my girl child working. Concentrate on your studies!" So I graduated from medical school debt free.

Even though I didn't get much academic credit for my year at the University of the West Indies, I was still able to get my bachelor's degree after only two years plus a sum-

Noreen around age 17 in the front yard of Trinidad home. Always meticulously dressed and pressed.

Haywood in Los Angeles, California, 1979

Mama—
Elsie L. Robinson, 1997

Noreen and
Haywood at
Noreen's OBGYN
residency
graduation dinner
in Los Angeles,
California, 1981

Wedding Day—Noreen and Haywood
in Los Angeles, California, 1981

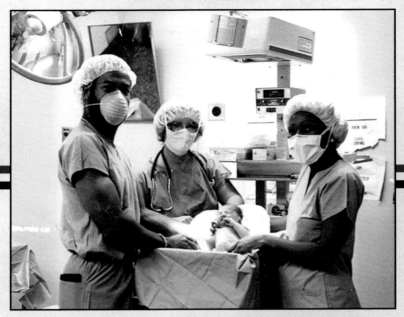

Noreen's first delivery in Bryan/College Station, Texas, 1981

Noreen and
Haywood,
Vancouver, BC,
Canada, 1986

From left: Dr. Stuart Quartemont, MD, Noreen and Haywood, and in purple, Gail Jackson, MD, in Oweeri, Nigeria, 2000

Haywood, Virginia, Udelle, Riva, and Noreen—spring break, Tahoe, California, 2000

Udelle with Kaishauna holding Riva in Bryan, Texas, 1986

Reception Area, Touch Tobago Clinic
in Charlotteville, Tobago, 2007

Haywood, Riva, Noreen, and Ma Johnson
at Riva's graduation from Rice University
in Houston, Texas, 2008

Noreen and Haywood at ceremony celebrating the closing of Planned Parenthood in Bryan, Texas, 2013

Riva, Kaishauna, and Udelle at Kaishauna's graduation from Texas A&M College of Medicine in Bryan, Texas, 2016

40 Days for Life,
Cape Town,
South Africa, 2018

Haywood and Noreen in
front of Mega Abortuary
in Houston, Texas, 2019

Haywood speaking
at a 40 Days for Life
Prayer Campaign, 2018

Haywood speaking at San Francisco Walk for Life, 2020

My 1951   Noreen 2021

"My Noreen" plaques on the Ebenezer Memorial Stone at 40 Days for Life Headquarters in Bryan, Texas

Haywood, November, 2021

mer semester at Howard. I had already been accepted into Howard's medical school, and I was determined to get my bachelor's before I started. I graduated *summa cum laude.*

My brother Royce didn't go to church. He married a Catholic lady but didn't actually convert to Catholicism until late in life, just before his heart transplant. He was never a churchgoer either, even though his wife went regularly to Mass. It was so much easier when I lived in DC to follow my brother's example in this, so while I lived there, I didn't go to church either. Except for my own personal knowledge of the Lord, I had no relationships that encouraged me in my spiritual life—no Christian friends, no fellowship groups, no church. That was true, too, at the University of the West Indies, before I left Trinidad. Once I moved out of my parents' home, I had no Christian fellowship at all. I was thoroughly immersed in the world.

Fast forward several years to when Haywood and I were married and living in College Station, Texas, and Haywood had his conversion experience at the Leon Patillo concert. Ironically, Haywood didn't say a word to me about what he'd experienced at the concert, but at the same time, he couldn't hide that *something* had changed. His behavior had changed, his attitudes had changed—when the foundation of your entire life has changed, that is obvious to anyone who's paying attention, and as his wife, I was paying attention. When you get saved, you get saved. As I watched him go through his transformation, I knew exactly what it was. My spiritual life may have been dormant for many years, and my professional activities as an abortionist may have pushed it even further into the background, but I had known, as a child, what it was like to have the Lord in my life. From about the time I was twelve until the time I left to go to college at around eighteen, I was serious about my relationship with the Lord. I was walking with Him. I didn't have the depth of Bible study and discipleship that Haywood would go through over the next few years, his first years as a believer. I really had no formal Bible study at all.

When it became clear to me that Haywood had turned his life over to the Lord and was diligently exploring all that that meant, it awakened a desire in me to recapture the intimacy and joy of that close relationship with the Lord. What was happening in Haywood's life had once been familiar to me, and dear. I began to feel a powerful hunger for the presence of God in my life again.

Haywood's transformation was very visible. For one thing, he went out and bought a Bible. And he would take it with him when he left the house early in the morning to meet with a group of men to pray. My husband—getting up *early* to go meet with a group of men to *pray*? Carrying a *Bible*?

And for another thing, a week after the concert, the same six-pack of Heineken was still sitting in the refrigerator, untouched! Believe me, *that* was different for Haywood.

Before that concert, I'm not sure we even had a Bible in the house. If there was, we could not have told you where it was. It certainly was not a part of our life. But when Haywood bought one and began to go off to Bible study or prayer early in the morning, I wanted to be able to read the Bible and enjoy fellowshipping with the Lord on my own during that time. So I bought a Bible too. And the Lord started speaking to me through His Word.

We have been fortunate in that we've always enjoyed a beautiful relationship. But even that relationship, our personal interaction, changed in ways I could not have imagined—in fact, *everything* changed about it. As physicians, we are very open about the body. We both understand the functions of the body and all of its parts, male and female. And yet even our sex life changed in surprising ways. Our physical encounters with each other became spiritual. It was a different level of intimacy.

All of this was before we started back to church. There was a gap between the time Haywood got saved and the time we started going to church, because I had a baby in the meantime—Riva. By c-section. So it was probably about two months after his encounter with the Lord that we went to church together for the first time, and we went to Aldersgate.

There is a coda to this chapter—it concerns something that took place many years after I moved away from Trinidad, shortly after I married Haywood and moved to Texas, but before the Leon Patillo concert or any of the events at Aldersgate. And it involves my sister Arlene.

In the years since she'd had her first abortion, Arlene had led a tumultuous life. And she'd had other abortions.

She had, however, kept one of her pregnancies and had given birth to her beloved son, Burt.

Arlene came from Trinidad to see me in Texas. "Noreen, I'm pregnant," she said. "And I'm too old to be having a baby. Plus I'm not married. I can't keep this baby, Noreen—and I know you do abortions. I need you to do an abortion on me before I go back to Trinidad. I trust you to do this, and I want to keep this between sisters. This is why I came all this way."

Could I do one on my own sister?

In the end, I decided if I was providing an important service for women I didn't even really know in their time of need, I would be a hypocrite if I didn't do one on my sister when she asked. So I did.

Somehow, when I performed that abortion, I never anticipated the phone call I would get from Arlene years later. "Noreen," she said. "Burt's dead. I've lost my son."

Burt, who had been her only living child, was now dead, killed in a freak boating accident. Of her pregnancies that had ended in abortion, the most recent one I had performed myself. I could blame it on her own promiscuity and irresponsibility, and there would be truth in that. But I knew the real truth—my sister was now without a living child because of me.

CHAPTER 9

A Crisis
of Conscience

Noreen

After Haywood's concert conversion and the visit from Calvin and Sarajane, Haywood and I decided that we should start to attend church. We'd visited three or four churches when we first came to College Station. Interestingly, we'd only visited Black churches. It never occurred to us to try a church outside our own ethnicity. Now, after our conversation with Calvin, one of us said, "So why don't we just go to Aldersgate?" It was, after all, the church where Haywood had responded to Leon's challenge, the place where he'd stood up to get things 100 percent right with God. Both of us liked Pastor Terry and Kay. Aldersgate, affiliated with the United Methodist Church, behaved like no other church of that denomination we'd ever visited or even heard of. It was cutting edge. It was, however, a predominantly white church, but we decided there was no reason that should stop us from giving it a try.

It was about two months after the Leon Patillo concert when I went to church with Haywood at Aldersgate for the first time. In the interim I had given birth to our daughter Riva, via C-section—so I had to recover from surgery. But that day turned out to be a day like no other in our lives, a day that would change many things.

At Aldersgate, I noticed right away that this church did worship differently than my momma's Baptist church from my childhood back in Trinidad, and from the youth group I attended when I lived with my brother Frank. For one thing, in my limited experience with church as a kid, I'd only heard and sung songs out of a hymnal. We sat down in Aldersgate the first Sunday morning and I thought, *Where are the hymnals?* At this church, they sang worship songs, and a great variety of them. And as we got into the service, I discovered that worship songs were all right with me. In fact, the praise and worship were so sweet that I couldn't imagine a more fertile setting for my heart to come alive to God again. People's hands were raised, their eyes were closed, and singing those beautiful worship songs brought us together as one. It was all new to Haywood too, of course, because since finishing high school, he had stayed away from church. I could tell that he was eager to engage in the spirit of worship as fully as those surrounding us were. After all, music and movement had always been his "thing." He had probably never heard most of Aldersgate's worship songs before his conversion. But then, neither had I. It would not be an overstatement to say I was blown away.

Another difference we noticed immediately was that, at Aldersgate, people were dressed informally—men in jeans, say, and a polo shirt. The churches we'd attended previously had encouraged their parishioners to dress more formally, like in a jacket and tie for men and a nice dress for women. We learned that this movement toward the casual had been happening at many churches in California for years—Calvary Chapel, for instance—but it still wasn't widely accepted in United Methodist churches in Texas.

Most people have never experienced such beautiful praise and worship as we experienced that morning. It's an experience that will draw you into God's presence. And being in the presence of the Lord, you can't help but be convicted of any stubborn sins remaining in your life.

I wasn't actually doing abortions in our practice at Brazos Medical Associates any longer by then. I had stopped some time before, and Haywood had never done them in Texas—he'd stopped when we left California. But when patients asked about the availability of abortion, we did what the American College of Obstetricians and Gynecologists recommends—we handed out a little trifold brochure that explains where abortions *can* be obtained, say in Austin or Houston.

When we came to church that day, unbeknownst to me, the Lord had been preparing me for the experience. After Haywood's conversion, I had been moved to start reading the Bible and setting aside some quiet time each day to renew my own relationship with the Lord. I needed to lie quietly toward the end of my pregnancy and as I recovered from the C-section. I certainly wasn't what I would call completely spiritually renewed—but I at least had gotten a start on some spiritual awakening—a few weeks' worth. My heart was well primed, when the opportunity arose, to come alive in the Holy Spirit.

The Holy Spirit didn't have to do much with me to get me convicted of my sin of engaging in abortion. I was primed. Immersed in the music, in the swaying, in the clapping, in the beauty of the words and the beauty of the voices singing those wonderful melodies, it all came to me in a matter of seconds.

The message that day had been an ordinary message. Nothing about the taking of innocent life. But even during the message, the Lord had placed on me—and on Haywood too—a deep spirit of conviction about our involvement in abortion. It was there during the message, and during the time of worship and praise afterward, it became so powerful, so irresistible. We'd had no conversation about this up to that point, we hadn't planned it. We hadn't entered the church that morning with this in mind. But once the pull of God toward the altar began, there was no denying it. Late in the service, I grabbed his hand and said, "Haywood, we need to go up to the altar and pray and ask God to forgive us for our sins ... for our involvement with abortion." *Our* sins, because I was well aware that I was the one who had introduced Haywood to the world of abortion as a money-making proposition, and that I had done so for no better reason than my own greed. He would have to take responsibility for what he had done in response, but I had to take responsibility for pulling him into it.

Haywood wasn't surprised when I pulled him toward the altar. The conviction was on him as well. Holding hands, we walked up to the altar and fell on our knees before the Lord. We prayed and we wept for our sins and for the damages done to families by our actions, for the lives that never had a chance to be realized.

Two women, Dawn Percival and Nancy Coen, came up and knelt beside us. Dawn had a ministry of prayer—she had been praying for us even before we got saved. She was gentle and softspoken and comforting. Nancy was outgoing and outspoken and prayed with great boldness. Neither Dawn nor Nancy nor any of the others who gathered around us to support us in prayer that morning had any idea why we were so repentant, so broken. They didn't know that it had anything to do with abortion. But they knelt with us and prayed.

Neither Haywood nor I had ever experienced anything remotely like this before. In Mark 15:39, at Jesus' crucifixion, as darkness settled over the earth and as, at the moment Jesus' earthly body died, the temple's curtain was ripped in two, from top to bottom, the Roman centurion who had stood in front of the cross throughout the ordeal said, "Surely this man was the Son of God." As a Roman soldier, his loyalty was to the Roman empire. On that morning, he was the leading officer with authority over all the soldiers carrying out the death sentence of Jesus. Then the Holy Spirit revealed to him who Jesus really was, and he could no longer deny what he was experiencing. God was working in his life. And that morning in church, kneeling at the altar, was for

Haywood and me our "centurion moment." We finally recognized, after killing all those preborn babies, after being dehumanized and desensitized, what the Lord was saying to us, and like the centurion, we cried out, "Oh, God!"

It was an encounter with the living God, stunning in its power. And we wept.

It was heartbreaking. Heartrending. We were aware of our blood-stained hands—but we also believed that Jesus could wash them clean. Kneeling there that morning in amazement opened up to us some small window into how God really feels about babies, the depth and unbelievable power of His love for the least of these, for those who are powerless to act on their own behalf. And despite the pain of the sorrow we felt, we also felt His forgiveness for our shameful pasts.

Haywood

Once we started attending Aldersgate Church, we recognized that the Holy Spirit continued working, even through the ways the service varied from week to week. Nowadays that doesn't seem so strange—but at the time, it was one of the things that made Aldersgate an odd fit in its denomination, not well liked by the established United Methodist ecclesiastical order. At the time, Methodist churches were still expected to be liturgical, to encourage more formality in their selection of music and dress on Sundays.

When we started at Aldersgate, there were only two or three other Black families. But over the years since, the church has become much more diverse, with increased numbers of Blacks and especially Hispanics. It has been a blessing to watch God's people of different ethnicities worshipping in a way befitting their own culture and style.

Occasionally, Aldersgate had a woman playing percussion on the worship team when we started attending there. She left the church before we'd been there long, and somehow I ended up sitting in with the worship team on tambourine. Gradually, I added a few more percussion instruments. By about 1988, I had become the full-time percussionist with the praise and worship group, and I still am.

The style of worship at Aldersgate was so different from my limited exposure to church. Once Noreen and I began to experience this together, we developed new friendships with people who reached out to us. People who were instrumental in building us up as new Christians. Some of them we still know and worship with today. Sometimes, with those new friends, we would have prayer vigils on Friday evening that would start at about seven o'clock and sometimes last until midnight. I would never have thought that I could sit around in a circle with a bunch of people, maybe one of us with a guitar leading praise, and pray—and enjoy it—for three or four hours. Are you kidding me? This was all so new. And so wonderful.

Noreen

Shortly thereafter, we dedicated Riva to the Lord at Aldersgate Church and asked Calvin to be her godfather. He and Sarajane knew of our involvement with abortion and had been praying for our salvation and deliverance for over a year.

The night of the dedication, after an intense time of prayer and fellowship at our home with Pastor Terry, Kay, Calvin, and Sarajane, I had an encounter with the Holy Spirit. The Bible talks about signs and wonders that follow those who believe, and I believe that's what I experienced that night. My heart was so warmed by an outpouring of God's love that I was lying on the sofa basking in God's presence when the telephone rang. It was Labor and Delivery. One of my patients had just shown up at twenty-three weeks in premature labor and was almost ready to deliver. Babies born at that stage are sometimes referred to as late spontaneous abortions. At that time a baby so premature was not considered a candidate for resuscitation because the likelihood of survival was so low.

I rushed to the hospital and found the baby partially delivered by the nurse. I completed the breech delivery, but the Apgar score (a scoring based on vital signs and activity of a newborn and how well it's surviving on its own outside the womb) was zero, meaning no heartbeat. I frantically applied all of my medical knowledge of resuscitation, trying to elicit a heartbeat, but the Apgar score remained at zero. After three minutes of futile efforts, it was as if I heard an almost-audible voice say, "Just lay your hands on that baby and pray." I obeyed.

There I stood, second after precious second for a full minute. That's when the baby hit the four-minute point—and I heard the nurse say, "Heart rate at ninety." I was so excited at the progress that I stopped praying and resumed my attempts to resuscitate, hoping to get the heart rate above 120. Instead, the heart rate plummeted again, back down to sixty at five minutes.

Was God trying to teach me a lesson? If so, I was ready for the final exam. I stopped all resuscitation and this time prayed aloud boldly, with words coming from my mouth that I did not recognize—but my spirit did. I prayed with my hand on that baby until at ten minutes the nurse said, "Heart rate above 120 and holding!" The baby was transferred to the nursery and I returned to care for the mother.

I knew I'd had a supernatural visitation, and my faith was boosted.

Another faith builder came some time after that incident. Amniocentesis is usually performed between sixteen and twenty weeks if genetic anomalies are suspected. The procedure requires inserting a spinal needle through the abdomen into the womb, guided by an ultrasound, to obtain amniotic fluid from around the baby for testing. As with any medical procedure, there are risks—in this case, the risk of injury to the baby or even possible death. To avoid that, it's important (via ultrasound) to see that the needle is away from the umbilical cord, baby, and placenta, and also to verify fetal movement and cardiac activity visibly and audibly before and after the procedure.

One day while performing an amniocentesis I was having great difficulty with proper needle placement. After my failed second attempt at obtaining fluid, my third and final needle insertion aspirated blood instead of clear fluid, and I panicked. I felt as if I was literally sweating blood. I heard an almost-audible voice, in a somewhat chastising tone, saying,

"What are you doing in here?" The meaning was crystal clear to me. God was asking me why I was tampering with His creation.

I immediately withdrew the needle and frantically picked up the ultrasound probe to check for fetal movement and the baby's heartbeat. After what seemed an eternity, thank God, both were present!

That was the last amniocentesis I ever performed. I now refer to them as "search and destroy missions."

Haywood

Reflecting on our experience at Aldersgate that Sunday morning when the Lord called us to repentance, I realize now that God doesn't allow the weight of your wrongs to descend fully upon you until He has, first, injected the reality of Jesus into your life and second, placed the Body of Christ around you to provide needed support. In other words, until He has a solution in place for your redemption, for your deliverance, and for your transformation.

Even though the Lord could have revealed to us at any time the gravity of our sin, say on a day when we were driving to the abortion facility to perform abortions, He chose to convict us of those sins with great power through the ministry of the Holy Spirit while we were in the company of a wonderful body of believers to support us. At the time I was performing abortions in California, I wasn't a believer, so the two-way line of communication wasn't yet open (although that didn't stop Him from challenging Saul on the road to Damascus!).

And if I had died during that period, before I came to Christ, it would not have been my activities as an abortionist that sent me to hell, over and above any other sin—it would have been not having as my Savior Christ who redeemed me from not just abortion but all other sins I had committed, throughout my life.

Is abortion a great sin, a great violation against the sanctity of life? Yes. But I believe it was precisely because abortion is so evil that God did not expose us to the magnitude of our evil until He had positioned us in a time and place that would provide the way for our healing. Until He had called us back to Himself and positioned us in a loving, Spirit-led church, we were not ready. That's how God works. He doesn't appear to you before you're saved and say, "Let Me tell you how much your killing these babies hurts Me. I'm about to cause you to be in a car accident and send you through the windshield to your death."

Why didn't God act sooner? Why didn't He compel us to come to Him before we'd performed abortions on all those women? Why couldn't He have saved me when I was twenty-five years old? And why couldn't I have been like Eloise and pushed back against the doctors during my residency who wanted to initiate me into the fraternity of the abortion cartel?

I can't tell you. I don't know.

Maybe it was the same reason He waited to reveal Himself to Saul until Saul had first imprisoned or killed many Christians.

All of the experiences we go through—injury, illness, or some other challenge—are for a purpose. And part of that purpose is to create a testimony, a story, that makes us into the person God desires us to be in order to fulfill His purposes in our life. To cause us to grow in Christian character.

We serve a gentle God. His way of dealing with us is usually not beating us over the head with our sin or rubbing our nose in it. Instead, when we confess our sins as Noreen and I did that morning at Aldersgate, He says, "I forgive you. That's over now—that sin is cast as far as the east is from the west. Now here's what we're going to do. You're in My program now. You're no longer a slave to the past. You're a new creature, transformed, and the only significance of that past sin now is that it was a springboard to a new life on earth and eternity in heaven."

Noreen has called abortion a cancer, one that is having a profound effect—not only on individual lives, but on families, on society, on the world at large.

Who is most affected by the cancer of abortion? It would be hard to argue that anyone else is more affected than the aborted preborn child. The baby loses everything—the life he never got a chance to experience outside the womb. Beyond that, a number of individuals are powerfully affected in their own way. The mother is affected physically, mentally, emotionally, spiritually, and psychologically. She may reserve a place in her heart for that aborted child for the rest of her life, just as she might have for a child that died by accident or illness, or that was stillborn. Depending on the role her husband or boyfriend played in pressing her toward having the abortion, that relationship might be damaged, even terminally. Or perhaps the father didn't want the child aborted. Maybe it was the mother's decision. He may well grieve that loss as powerfully as a mother would.

Consider the effect on the physician. We wrote earlier about how, for the doctor, initiation into the world of abortion is a process of desensitization, of dehumanization. The first procedure may be jarring. The second, less so, and so on—until the doctor, if he or she has retained enough humanity, is in a full-blown crisis of conscience, as Noreen and I were that morning at Aldersgate.

Families have secrets, and for the most part those secrets are destructive. We have tried to be transparent about the effects of our time as abortionists on our lives and our family, but some of those effects have sometimes been kept secret. In every family, there are some things we just don't like to talk about. Abortion. Incest. Infidelity. Addiction. We sweep them under the carpet, hide them in the closet. Unless we deal with these issues head on, recognize them, confront them, and dispose of them with God's help, they will remain a cancer and continue to wreak havoc within the family and beyond.

The first time Noreen or I performed an abortion or even saw one—that was stage I of the cancer of abortion. This is why Noreen and I now tell medical students when we mentor them, "Don't even accept the invitation to go into that room. You don't want to see one." Watching the abortion being performed is a type of desensitization. It's like saying to a teenage boy, "I have a little bit of pornography here I'd like you to see. Just a little—it's all right, it won't hurt you.

I just want you to know what's out there so you can make an informed decision. There—you see? You looked at it and survived!" That's how the desensitization begins. See enough of them, and then it's no big deal. But it should be.

If, let's say, someone had come to us after our first abortion, challenged what we were doing and pointed out the contradictions inherent in a doctor who has sworn an oath nevertheless performing an operation in which, by design, a human being will die, we might have become aware that what we were doing was wrong. We might have stopped that cancer in our lives at stage I.

But what does a cancer want to do? It wants to metastasize, to spread through the body. If the doctor continues to practice abortion, that cancer takes over more of his heart and mind. It becomes easier. It ceases to have any relationship to the thought of taking a unique human life. As Noreen and I engaged in abortions for the purpose of making extra money, we were at risk. We allowed that cancer to reach stage II or maybe even stage III in our lives.

Inevitably, for the physician who continues to practice abortion over time, it colors every part of their humanity, and when that happens, the cancer has become fully metastatic. Doctors like Leroy Carhart who performs late-term abortions are at stage IV—but at least as of this writing, he's still alive, and as long as someone still lives, there's hope for repentance.

Look at the cancer another way—from the viewpoint not of the physician but of the family. When Noreen's sister Arlene had her first abortion at age seventeen or eighteen, let's call that stage I. But that cancer of abortion was never treated. Its effects were visible in the family for anyone who looked: Noreen was sent off to live with her brother Frank so that her young heart wouldn't be "polluted" by a misbehaving sister. Ma Johnson was persecuted by an angry husband.

The cancer was growing.

Little did Noreen know that she was getting the cancer too. She fell in love with medicine—specifically, women's medicine—and no sooner had she gotten her license to practice medicine than that cancer showed up in her, and she began to perform the same procedure that had nearly destroyed her own family when she was a child.

And then she gave it to me!

No, I'm not blaming her for that. My own choice. I'm just connecting the dots so that you can see that once that cancer has taken hold in a family, it continues to metastasize.

Noreen has said, "Abortion made its impact on me starting with Arlene's first abortion. I was thirteen or fourteen. And I swore I would never be sexually active outside marriage. I'd be a good girl. I thought I was too smart to do the things she had done and fall into the same trap that she fell into. Did I get pregnant before marriage? No. Did I become promiscuous like she did? No. But instead, I became an abortionist! And I asked another abortionist to abort my first pregnancy. The cancer was still there, still with a profound effect on my life."

We've described abortion as a cancer. Here's another way to look at it. The Niagara River starts out as a small stream that flows into Lake Erie. That small stream, near its headwaters, would seem pretty innocuous. You could step over it. But where it exits Lake Erie, it's a large-enough river to be threatening. And it gets even bigger. Think of Niagara Falls. I've seen it, and I said, "Where did *this much water* come from?"

In the same way: How did we get to more than fifty million babies killed by abortion on the planet annually? Or a million and a half babies killed in the United States every year?

It started with Cain killing his brother Abel, the first murder, which reduced the population of the planet by 25 percent. It started as a stream. And it continues with the enemy who whispers in the ear of frightened or desperate people whatever he needs to whisper to cause them to see aborting—killing—their own offspring as a desirable thing. He comes to steal, kill, and destroy.

That's what cancer does. It advances relentlessly, stealing your health, until it has destroyed your life.

CHAPTER 10

Wounded Souls Revived

Haywood

The Bible says, in 2 Corinthians 5:17 (NIV), "Therefore, if anyone is in Christ, the new creation has come: The old has gone, the new is here!" Even if I didn't feel that way the moment I walked out of the Leon Patillo concert at which I stood up to get myself 100 percent right with God, the changes in my life that came within the next few weeks had me feeling that way really quickly. Everything about my life was changing, and for the better.

It was precisely because of the power of those changes in my life, though, that I found myself feeling angry with the church I'd grown up in back in California. I was baptized in that church as an infant. Since we rarely traveled anywhere, I accompanied Mama and my brother there every Sunday until I left for college when I was seventeen years old. And I never heard the gospel message? What's up with that? I was not only angry, I was disillusioned. The church leaders I'd looked up to all those years, surely some of them must have known the message of the cross. Did they not think it important enough to share with the church at large? Did they not believe it?

Or had the devil just stuck a pair of earplugs in me every time I went to church?

Looking back, I think that at our church, attending was a social event rather than a spiritual one. People liked to get dressed up and greet their friends. *Oh, those are such cute shoes! Where did you get them? And what a great-looking suit!*

My brother and I liked getting dressed up as much as anyone else did, believe me. Mama definitely knew how to dress, and when she would take Howard and me out to buy clothes, even though we didn't have a lot of money, from the time we two were thirteen or fourteen we went to nice shops and bought expensive clothes. We never looked at the price tags. Irrelevant. We had good taste and wanted the best, and Mama bought it for us.

That taste for quality things was one of the things that drove me. Fortunately, I assumed, the profession I had chosen would enable me to afford the things I liked, would enable me to move to an area of nicer homes, nicer stores, cleaner streets—I didn't want to live any longer in the environment, in the community, that I'd grown up in. I didn't want to live like that anymore.

But that wasn't the only reason I decided as a child that I wanted to become a doctor.

Eventually, I had to let go of some of that quasi-bitterness toward my church. But I learned from it, too, and one thing

I learned was how many people go to church every Sunday who for one reason or another never hear the gospel. There are pastors who will have to stand before God and be held accountable for not preaching the gospel of Christ's death and resurrection and what it means for us. It's not going to be pretty for them.

I've mentioned going to church with my mother. My father not only didn't go to church with us, he didn't like my mother going either. He would tolerate it on Sunday mornings, but anything during the week—say an evening service on Sunday, or a mid-week prayer service, or youth group activities on the weekend—it wasn't happening. He didn't want her going, and if that's what he wanted, that's what happened.

My mother was an unbelievable seamstress. She used to make clothing for other ladies. But when those women would come to get measured and get their garments fitted, my father used to give Mama such a hard time that it was hardly worth it for her. He set major limits on all of us in the household as far as what we could do when, but particularly on Mama.

Mama didn't drive, and the idea of our dad driving us to some youth group activity, or driving Howard and me to visit some of our church friends our age—no way. So our connection to our church was attending Sunday school and church on Sunday mornings. That was it. And none of the kids from our church lived close enough for us to walk over to play with them.

So our friends, Howard's and mine, were the kids in the neighborhood. There were boys and girls all up and down our block that we played with. Those were my people. One of them—I call him Pedro—I met in November of 1962 and he's still a dear friend with whom I maintain contact.

In the first few months after my conversion and our repentance at Aldersgate, I grew spiritually. But Noreen had a term for it—she called it "fast and furious kindergarten-first grade Christianity." In other words, I was enthusiastic and I was getting the basics down. But no one would have mistaken my level of Christianity for a mature faith.

Even so, when we began attending some of the few pro-life conferences at the time, drawn there by our concern about abortion, when people in the movement would find out that we were former abortionists, that drew a lot of attention our way. People would say, "Do you have a card? Can I get your contact information? We'd love to have you come speak at one of our meetings."

One of the first invitations I accepted was to join the board of a new organization that had just opened in Bryan/College Station—the Brazos Valley Crisis Pregnancy Center. That became my main area of ministry for some time, and I served the center in a variety of positions over time. I was their first medical director, and in that role I brought ultrasound in as a service we offered. I was also involved with Operation Rescue, led locally by Rex Moses of Austin, Texas.

When we started, we had a budget of $1100 a month. We humans tend to place a lot of importance on size. We say, "Well, my church is small. Only a hundred members."

Or, "I attend a mega-church—we have four thousand people in three services every Sunday, and we're bursting at the seams!" Or, "Our offerings bring in enough cash that we support a dozen missionaries around the world." But remember: It's not about the numbers. It's about the power God gives even a small number of us (say, a dozen disciples) to change the world. I love the verse Zechariah 4:10 (THE MESSAGE): "Does anyone dare despise this day of small beginnings?" God loves to take small beginnings and see them grow, grow, grow. That same PRC that once had a monthly budget of $1100 is now called Hope Pregnancy Center. Last I heard it had a budget of about $300,000. So, from between $12,000 and $14,000 annually to $300,000—when you're walking with the Lord, you see the Word become flesh. The Word is alive. Now, when I read a scripture like, "Unless the LORD builds the house, the builders labor in vain" (Psalm 127:1 NIV), I know what that means! I've been watching that house get built.

Just a few months ago I was on a Zoom call to India, exploring possibilities for a new 40 Days for Life campaign in that country. (I am now the director of medical affairs and education for 40 Days for Life.) And over the course of the call, as I looked on my computer screen at all of those Indian faces looking at me live with such hope and expectation, I had a sudden sense of how the enemy perverts God's creativity. There was such diversity on display right there on my computer monitor. One of the leaders was Robert Calhoun, who's white, and I could see his picture. I could see my own picture. And a whole lot of other faces on the screen were dark-skinned—not African in heritage but rather southeast Asian, from India. What a great example of how God has, in His creativity, made all of us human beings for many thousands of years without ever making one of us exactly like another. And yet, as diverse as we are from one another, we're all made in his image.

Then along comes the devil and takes that very artistic and creative expression of God's, all those beautiful colors and shapes, and uses it to divide people. Racism. Sexism. Ageism.

In 1969, the original *Star Trek* series aired an episode entitled "Let That Be Your Last Battlefield." In that episode, the Starship Enterprise rescues a space traveler, Lokai, who is human in appearance but whose skin is black on the left side of his body and white on the right. Not long after, another space traveler beams aboard, his skin white on the *left* side of his body and black on the *right*, just the opposite of Lokai. It turns out that both of them are from the planet Cheron, and their two races—each half black and half white, but on opposite sides of their bodies—have been waging bitter warfare for tens of thousands of years. In fact, the second traveler, Bele, has been pursuing Lokai across space for about fifty thousand earth years.

The two aliens from Cheron argue over the history of the conflict between their races and who's to blame. Bele gains control of the Enterprise and diverts it to Cheron—but when they arrive, Spock, using the ship's sensors, is unable to locate any intelligent life on the entire surface of the planet.

Bele and Lokai are forced to conclude that their warlike races have utterly destroyed each other and their entire civilization in their mindless rage in the tens of thousands of years since the two warriors departed. The two attack each other and beam down to the surface of Cheron. The episode ends with the Enterprise's bridge staff regretting the Cheron civilization's eagerness to destroy each other over something as insignificant as differences in patterns of skin pigment.

But what struck me most when I first saw the episode wasn't that final discussion among Kirk and Spock and the others about the lack of importance of skin pigment. It was the *look on Spock's face* when they all first realized that the two main races of Cheron's civilization had destroyed themselves and each other over it, and Lokai and Bele, rather than mourning the loss and calling a truce, set out to finish the battle once and for all. It's as if Spock were saying, "All this over whether the black and the white are on the left or the right? Can't they see it makes no difference?"

People still debate whether "Let That Be Your Last Battlefield" was one of the great episodes of *Star Trek*. Whether it was or not, it has been ranked one of the top ten episodes of the series with regard to tolerance, and the episode struck with enough power that I think it caused a lot of people to say, "Yeah, I get it now."

Our nation still struggles mightily with racial divisions, and one place we definitely saw no reason for racial divisions was within the pro-life movement. But the more involved we got with that movement, the more we wondered where the Blacks were, the people who looked like us. Noreen and I saw the swelling tide of abortions across the world as a holocaust, and we thought surely there must be more Blacks who agreed with us. The pro-life movement was predominantly being led by white people, which makes sense on one level. There are, after all, more whites than Blacks in the country. But it's also true that, depending on whose figures you believe, Black women are obtaining abortions at a rate about twice as high as their white counterparts.

This is the result of policies shaped by Margaret Sanger, eugenics, and racism pursued by some for decades. This woman founded the American Birth Control League that became Planned Parenthood.

Were there other Black people of like mind? We began seeking them out. But at first we felt like Elijah in the desert in 1 Kings 19, fleeing from Ahab, when he said, "'I am the only one left, and now they are trying to kill me too'" (verse 10). It turns out he was just feeling sorry for himself—and just a few verses later, God told him (in the Haywood Standard Version), "'Hold it! Hold it! I've still got seven thousand in Israel—and none of them have yet bowed down to Baal'" (see verse 18). As with Elijah, it turned out Noreen and I weren't the only ones serving.

First, we found out that two Black ladies, Juliet and Akua, would be speaking at Texas A&M in the MSC—Memorial Student Center. We went—and these were two fierce women! They were fire-breathers! I said, "Whoa! Noreen, we've gotta meet these two!" It turned out they were from Houston, just a short drive from Bryan/College Station. So we drove down and met them, and they were able to suggest others we should meet. Soon we knew Black pro-lifers from Indiana, Missouri, New York, and elsewhere. Soon we called all of them we knew—about fifteen at that point—to spend some time with us at the Hilton in Houston. It wasn't seven thousand, or even seven hundred, but it was a start. And don't despise small beginnings!

Since we seemed to be forming an organization, we needed a name. We thought about Black Americans for Life, but it turned out that name was already in use by another group.

Any discussion, I think, of the Black pro-life movement has to start with Johnny Hunter. You could call him the professor emeritus of the Black pro-life movement. You could call him its founder. The Reverend Doctor Johnny Hunter of Fayetteville, North Carolina. He's been right there with us from the start, teaching, encouraging, etc.

Twenty or so years ago, we had an organizational meeting in Houston of Black pro-life leaders, and that's where we officially created the organization that still exists today, and where we came up with a name for it: LEARN—Life Education and Resource Network, based in Fayetteville, where Johnny Hunter lives. He's the National Director and I'm chairman of the board. It's the largest Black, evangelical, pro-life ministry in the US. The largest—but not the only one. Another organization is the Issues4Life Foundation, founded by Rev. Walter B. Hoye, II. Another is LEARN Northeast, in Montclair, New Jersey, founded by Rev. Clenard Childress, Jr., who is the current director.

Most of those organizations have resources available, and you can learn a lot just by scanning their websites. One thing you're frequently reminded of on those websites: Abortion is the number-one killer of African-Americans. It outnumbers the next three causes combined, all by itself. The most dangerous place for a Black person in America is a Black womb.

Noreen

Once we became known as ex-abortionists who had turned to the pro-life cause, we were invited to speak at many different venues. In this way, we gained national and international exposure that introduced us to a great many more people in the pro-life world. We spoke both together and individually in countries like Chile, Nicaragua, Jamaica, and Trinidad.

As an OBGYN, I also was called on occasion to provide expert testimony in states where some lawmakers were attempting to liberalize abortion laws—states such as Louisiana and Florida. In Florida, in fact, one late-term abortionist who is still on my prayer list, Dr. Pendergraft, was testifying before a legislative committee trying to open up the state to abortions in the second and even third trimester. He had a number of abortion facilities in Florida and was at the time attempting to open one in Orlando. I was asked to come down and testify before the committee about the dangers of abortion in general but specifically about late-term abortion. Many of the legislators lacked knowledge of late-term abortion procedures, a lack I was there to remedy.

We spent a lot of time on the road then, speaking at a number of pro-life venues—such as the American Life League. We also attended a couple of the early March for Life events in DC.

It starts in the heart. Once renewed by the Holy Spirit, a cold heart warms up and beats to a new drumbeat. I understand now what Jesus meant when He told Nicodemus, "You must be born again." With a warm and renewed heart, I could see people through the eyes of God. Where there was suffering, I could see that suffering. When compassion was needed, I could feel compassion. I discovered a driving instinct to heal the broken-hearted, to preach good news to the poor, and to proclaim liberty to the captives behind prison doors. That was what Jesus was called to do, and as His followers who are challenged to pattern our lives after His, it is what we are called to do too.

Because we found ourselves thrust into ministry very soon after our conversion, we were at risk—even if we didn't know it at the time. Believers caught in that position, launched into ministry while still spiritually immature and maybe overzealous, are at risk of falling victim to the enemy. How do you avoid that? It's important to maintain a steady diet of discipleship and mentoring for proper spiritual growth. Haywood and I were fortunate to have a biblically sound church and pastor and to be surrounded by many others who supported us and reached out to us after salvation.

One key figure for Haywood and me during that period was Dr. Philip Ney, a Canadian psychiatrist, psychotherapist, psychoanalyst, author, and teacher who served as a mentor for us both spiritually and concerning abortion. He was the founder of Centurions, an organization that ministers to medical professionals who have escaped the abortion industry. Philip Ney firmly believes that abortion has a long reach into the family and society. His psychotherapy is based on that belief.

He invited us to travel with him as he ministered to former abortion workers and providers in Eastern Europe after the collapse of the Soviet Union. And although we ministered alongside him, in reality we were being ministered *to* just as much. It was Philip, on that trip, who helped us unravel some of the pieces that, psychologically and spiritually, had been holding us back. He helped us really examine what we had done in those years we had been performing abortions.

I was part of his team on another trip as well—to Ukraine. Even though I was there as part of his ministry team, I was also benefiting from his experience and wisdom by participating in all of the exercises. In other words, part of what I was there to do was to be healed—to do the hard work of facing up to my participation in abortion. In doing this, I was part of a small group, about ten of us, guilty of performing abortions and now seeking forgiveness and healing.

In performing abortions, not only had I become desensitized to the humanity of the preborn child and to the pain and suffering of the mother, but I had damaged myself as well—I had traded away much of my humanity for nothing more than the fee for performing abortions, just as Judas had traded his for thirty pieces of silver to betray Jesus. My heart had grown cold and callous.

One exercise Philip gave us was to go back to the very beginning. What were you like as a child? What do you think God's plan for your life was in the beginning? So, when my turn came to speak, I told about my upbringing in Trinidad and about my painful experience with Arlene and her first abortion, when I was a young teen.

Next, he had us write down our whole family tree and highlight those who were missing, either by death or by abortion. And in *my* family tree, of course, there was a highlighted space representing the aborted child of my sister Arlene that *I* was responsible for. Talking with him about that part of the homework forced me to examine very closely my role in the death of that child, in the opening up of an empty spot in our family tree. "To find closure in the matter of this child's death," Philip said, "you have to bury this child. You killed a child. You have to bury that child." And he had us go through a burial for the children we had killed as abortionists. This was so we could rehumanize the babies. Those babies had lost their humanity not only because we had killed them but because we had treated each of them as nothing more than individual blobs of tissue.

In order to rehumanize the babies, and so we could bury them, we had to name the babies. I named Arlene's Grace. My niece.

Every night Philip gave us a different assignment, all of them heartrending. During the day we were in the workshop, sharing openly (but confidentially) with each other. We grieved openly as well. And then we had to write about our experience. To walk through the steps of grief. And to write letters. Yes, I had to write a letter to Grace. I had to write a letter to my sister, asking for her forgiveness. I wrote a letter to my father because I was very angry with the way he had handled Arlene's abortion. And Philip walked us through all of these things.

During this whole process, I was barely able to sleep at night—and not only because of my grief and inner turmoil. It was cold in Ukraine—I don't remember what month it was, but maybe early spring. We were staying in an old monastery, not well heated. So, I stayed up partly because I was too cold and uncomfortable to fall asleep. And, being awake, I grieved. I cried. I read my Bible. Trying to do the assignments Philip had given us kept me awake, too. In order to name my niece, for instance, I had to visualize what she would have been like then, twelve years after she was aborted. Philip had us visualize our child from birth up until whatever their current age would have been. Then: What did I think she would have become if she had grown up? I envisioned Grace as going into public service, possibly as an ambassador, maybe from Trinidad to the United Nations. But I definitely saw her as a public figure. That was painful for me all through a sleepless night—and then we had to come back the next day, write it up, and go through it with the rest of the group.

One of the things I learned through all this was how important it is for mothers who have lost babies to grieve adequately. When a woman has a miscarriage, her grief is seen as normal, and she can grieve openly. When a woman has an abortion, she can't grieve openly. It's secret. But to really grieve appropriately and effectively, she has to rehumanize the baby, because in order for her to have the abortion in the first place, she convinced herself that the baby was not a person. That it was a blob of tissue, and not a baby who would look like her and its father, created in the image of God. To seek healing through grieving, you have to grieve a person. You can't grieve a blob of tissue.

Philip believes that if, after an abortion, you avoid grieving because it makes you feel guilty, you will suffer the consequences of suppressed grief. Then depression sets in. And the psychological consequences of abortion lead to physical consequences as well. Those could include disorders related to faulty immune responses. Cancer. Arthritis and related pain syndromes. A variety of infections. Difficultly getting pregnant again.

I think most women are pretty truthful with their doctors. They're often aware that there are physical consequences a woman might experience after an abortion. They might, when they talk to their doctor about some physical ailment after an abortion, say, "I had an abortion six months ago. Could this be related to that?" They're less likely to ask whether the psychological or behavioral changes they're experiencing might be related to the abortion: alcoholism, depression, lack of regard for life in general, including their own. Child abuse. Child neglect. All of those things could be connected.

Haywood and I were redeemed. We repented of the sin of abortion and committed to never performing them again. But there was still much healing to be done.

PART IV

The Mission

CHAPTER 11

The Birth of a Vision

Haywood

Around 1993, a man—a Christian man—owned some land on East 29th Street in Bryan, Texas. A company made him a good offer to buy that land for development. Unbeknownst to the seller, that company was the one that Planned Parenthood used to stealthily buy land on which to build their abortion facilities. Had he known that the land he was selling would be used for a Planned Parenthood facility, he would not have sold it to them.

I first heard that a Planned Parenthood facility was going to be built in our town from a friend, David Bereit. He was a pharmaceutical rep who would periodically call on me at my office—an incredibly likeable fellow. He knew I was a believer, as was he, so once we would finish with his marketing responsibilities, the conversation always turned to family and faith. Over time we'd become good friends and would sometimes have breakfast together. He knew the story of my past and I knew he was pro-life, so when he broke the news to me about Planned Parenthood, we were both extremely concerned.

I felt particularly frustrated by the sneaky way they went about purchasing the property, but I wasn't surprised. I, probably better than most, knew firsthand how incredibly lucrative the abortion business is. It felt personal to me—like an encroachment on our territory, our town. They had snuck in to steal, kill, and destroy the next and future generations for the almighty dollar. I perceived a threat. I was offended. And I felt protective. I'd long resented their clever use of their name to indicate they were all about "family planning" when in reality they were all about revenue. Their very name is a lie. More accurately stated, it should be Planned Deparenthood.

When word spread around town, there was quite a stir among the pro-life community—which, at that time, consisted predominantly of Catholics. The pregnancy resource center had already been established at that time, and David and I were already active with it, as were a good many other people, and we were all stunned. We had no doubt that, for Planned Parenthood, the appeal of Bryan/College Station was the presence of Texas A&M and a whole bunch of sexually active young people with frequent unplanned pregnancies.

One of the local women who heard about the coming of Planned Parenthood and felt that we needed to do something about it was Lauren Gulde, an undergrad at A&M. Unsure of herself and afraid that her effort would be rejected or fruitless, she nevertheless stepped out in faith and called a meeting at Saint Mary's Catholic Church to discuss the coming of Planned Parenthood and what, if anything, could be done about it. Noreen and I both decided to go—this was, after all, something that we had some history with and some knowledge of.

Lauren called people together not on behalf of some organization, but only as an expression of righteous indignation and passion. There was no statement of mission or objective. This was strictly an informal, unofficial, grassroots response. Lauren simply sent out word calling together people of like mind, asking, *What are we going to do about this?*

We were amazed when we arrived at the church that night to find the place packed. I heard later that over four hundred people from a variety of churches attended. I didn't speak at the meeting, nor did Noreen. My friend David Bereit was there, of course. He was already fervently committed to the pro-life cause, but he didn't speak either. Lauren spoke. I seem to recall that the priest spoke also. And even though we had come together with no clear objective, there were a couple of decisions that came out of the meeting: First, that we would get together again and continue to try to find ways to fight this, and second, that we would come together at the prospective site of the Planned Parenthood facility on 29th Street and pray.

Other than that, frankly, we didn't have any idea of what we were going to do. How does one oppose the building of something like this?

Our local doctors had an idea. None—or very few—of

them were in favor of the idea of Planned Parenthood coming to town, so when the new facility was announced, a sizeable group of local doctors (at least a hundred) took out a full-page ad in *The Eagle*, our local newspaper. It read something like, "We the undersigned doctors of the Brazos Valley want to register our extreme disapproval of the opening of a Planned Parenthood abortion facility ..." and so on, with all of our names clearly displayed, along with a big picture of a baby.

Our informal little group of pro-lifers tried a few things. One was to talk to subcontractors that the general contractor planned to use and warn them that if they were to work on this Planned Parenthood building, it could affect their businesses. That helped—it slowed things down a bit. But not enough. The building was completed and Planned Parenthood opened in Bryan, Texas.

At their grand opening, Noreen and I and many other active pro-lifers were standing on the sidewalk out in front of their building praying. Demonstrating in that way was new and uncomfortable for many of us. Most didn't have backgrounds in civil disobedience, in protests, in political or social activism.

For Noreen and me, it became even more uncomfortable, and more personal, as we stood there on the sidewalk praying that morning and a Jaguar pulled out of the parking lot onto the street. As it passed, we made eye contact with the driver. "Isn't that ..." I started to say. It was our neighbor, Ellen Benton. She saw us, too. She and her husband, Tom, were not just our neighbors but our good friends. We hung out together frequently and had great fun. Now, it turned out, she was on the Planned Parenthood local board. The Robinsons and the Bentons had ended up on opposite sides of this particular passionate life issue.

We showed up and made our presence felt that day, and that group that met at St. Mary's Catholic Church kept meeting. Eventually, they came up with a name: Brazos Valley Coalition for Life—BVCL. Lauren was its first executive director. And Noreen became one of the charter board members.

The Coalition for Life conducted a variety of efforts designed to combat Planned Parenthood. We would picket or pray in front of the Hilton when Planned Parenthood held its fundraiser. When they had events at board members' houses, we'd stand in front of their houses. But it was all unfocused and haphazard.

If for some of you, this account sounds somewhat familiar, that's not surprising. I'm describing the founding of 40 Days for Life, a pro-life organization many readers will be familiar with. That has been described in other places, but it's important for the purposes of *this* book to describe how Noreen and I became involved. So this is our personal account—the Robinson/Johnson version of the founding of 40 Days.

Soon, Lauren Gulde challenged David, who by that time was the director of BVCL: "You've been vacillating about whether maybe someday you should dive full time into the fight against abortion. Well—why don't you? Just do it."

And David did it.

What happened after that was a complete walk of faith for the Bereits. People in ministry, especially those in fledgling nonprofits, are low paid. But when the Bereits were in need of a car, a local guy who owned a car dealership gave him a car. When David and the Bereits needed support, he was able to get whatever support he needed. He never lost his stride. When Lauren Gulde got married and started having kids and didn't have the time to serve as director any longer, David stepped in as director.

Organizations have stages. Lauren had the original vision and gave BVCL its start. When David stepped in as director, boy, did that organization move to the next level. He's a master media specialist and a powerful speaker—the only guy I've ever heard speak for an hour and a half and seemingly not take a breath or even a drink of water.

A short time after that, David called me up, his voice almost quivering with excitement, and said, "Can you come to a meeting? We're going to be sharing something monumental."

"Sure," I said. I'd known David for a long time, and I knew that when he was this excited, it had to be about something really good. I'd been involved with BVCL; I'd participated in a few of their activities and I was ready to hear what David had to say about this one—whatever it was.

There were a lot of us who showed up that night—in fact, the place was packed out. We gathered around the now-famous conference table in their small conference room and, when everyone was there, David said, "The Lord has told us that we're about to launch a new program." First, he led us through a brief description of the many ways the number forty had shown up in Scripture. "We want to follow that pattern," he said finally. "Coalition for Life is going to have forty days of prayer and fasting in front of that facility right down the street. And it's going to start on ..." And he give us the date.

We all looked around at each other and said, "All right."

Frankly, it was such a new and revolutionary idea that we didn't know how to respond. Should we be afraid? Excited? But one thing I believe we all felt was hope. Up until now we'd been frustrated, feeling that nothing we were doing was making an impact in fighting Planned Parenthood. We believed in the Lord's leading, and in David, and we signed on—and signed up for particular dates and times.

Our plan was to hold a forty-day campaign that had three objectives: To dedicate ourselves to peacefully pray and fast for the end of abortion, and to reach out to the community inviting others to pray as well, and to hold a peaceful prayer vigil around the abortion facility every day for forty days.

We started at midnight on the first day, and I was there. At midnight. The other guy who'd signed up for that first night was Shawn Carney, a young guy I'd met for the first time not long before, thanks to David. In fact, David also began to bring Shawn to our breakfast meetings, now a weekly event. He didn't look old enough to be out of high school yet, let alone in college and working at a nonprofit like BVCL—and in fact he'd only been working there a few days when I met him. If the term "wet behind the ears" didn't already exist, we'd have had to invent it just for Shawn.

During that first forty-day campaign, we tried to keep good records. We watched ... and we counted. We knew what the usual flow of cars was into that parking lot. And to our excitement, we were able to document a 50 percent drop of cars coming in when we were praying there. Which meant a 50 percent drop in abortions—if pregnant women wouldn't come into the parking lot, then they couldn't have the abortion they'd planned to get. But we wanted to do our homework—we wanted to make sure. So we verified our findings with county abortion statistics. It wasn't just wishful thinking. We were able to demonstrate, by official unbiased county statistics, that when we do a 40 Days campaign, babies are saved.

Understand that this was early days. We hadn't thought as far ahead as seeing facilities closing or workers leaving the industry. We had a single-minded goal. But in pursuing that goal—yes, BVCL, through our 40 Days for Life campaign, was saving babies.

We thought we were onto something big, something good, but we wanted to be cautious and not get ahead of ourselves. So we waited until after we'd done two or three campaigns before we started to promote it nationally and look for partners to spread it to other cities.

One practical reason to be so cautious was: Marketing this new campaign would require some money. And we didn't want to ask for money until we could prove, unequivocally and objectively, "Look, here's what's going on in Bryan, Texas. When our volunteers stand on the sidewalks and pray, this happens. Here's the number of abortions performed before we started our prayer campaigns. Here's what the total number of abortions is now. And all we had to do was stand and pray. For twenty-four hours a day. For forty days."

The first campaign outside of Bryan was in Dallas. Then

Kitsap County, Washington. Then Houston, then Green Bay, Wisconsin. And it seemed like, from that point, it took no time for us to reach a total of about 588 sites internationally per campaign.

The early days of my relationship with the Coalition were informal. I had no official position or title—I was just there. I was always stopping by, poking my head in the door and seeing what was up, helping to plan and carry out some outreach, or something. And that was simply because I loved the organization and what they were doing. This was long before I came on staff.

After the first three years or so of running these 40 Days for Life campaigns as BVCL, the board decided we would change the name of the organization to 40 Days for Life and make those 40-day campaigns the primary focus of the organization. What better way, we thought, to communicate to pro-life groups and churches across the country—across the planet—that if you get the people in your city together to stand, pray, and fast, you will see the same outcomes that we have. Our name said it. This is what we do and what you can do too, and it will work. It was a simple model. It worked better in some places than others. But it worked. How much of it was due to the name change and how much to the simple fact that what we were doing worked, and we were willing to help other groups across the country and in many other countries do the same thing, I don't know, but our growth was stratospheric. It just blew up. But why should we be surprised? The Bible declares, "The effectual fervent prayer of a righteous man availeth much" (James 5:16, KJV). God does not lie! Of course, our prayers should work. And, be aware, abortion offends God far more than it does us. So get behind God and stop this holocaust.

Noreen

When our kids were tiny, we were only new believers. But we were determined to avoid as many mistakes as possible in raising our children, even though neither Haywood nor I had the benefit of consistently godly parenting when we were children, at least not from our fathers. Thank God, we raised two beautiful Christian girls.

Udelle always loved babies. She was always precocious. She begged to go to Montessori School when she was only two and a half years old—we think just to be around other kids. When we dropped her off at school the first day and she saw the other children, she ran off and never looked back at us.

As soon as Udelle could speak, she started asking us for a baby sister. In fact, I did get pregnant between the two girls, and miscarried at twelve weeks. It was Udelle who provided the best source of comfort when she saw my tears on my return home from having a D&C to clean up after the miscarriage. She said, "Don't cry, Mommy, you'll get another baby." A few months later I was pregnant with her baby sister, Riva.

Riva, so different from Udelle, informed us that she would go to school when she was five years old; until then she would stay at home with Grandma. True to her word, when she was five, Riva started preschool.

Our lives were busy. Thank God for Mama Robinson

who took care of our girls and ran our house. She was on call 24/7 whenever Haywood or I had to deliver a baby or respond to a medical emergency at the hospital, often both of us at the same time. That released us to work full time in our medical practices and simultaneously be heavily engaged in pro-life ministry.

When the announcement was made that Planned Parenthood would open an abortion facility in town, righteous indignation welled up. The Planned Parenthood facility opened regardless, and our little pro-life group, Brazos Valley Coalition for Life, began our simple strategy of peaceful, prayerful presence in front of the abortion facility day and night until the facility closed.

The medical community here in Bryan/College Station is supportive of 40 Days for Life and of the pro-life movement in general. The doctors here are predominantly Christian and many of them are donors, either to 40 Days for Life or to other pro-life organizations. I'm reminded of what Dr. Benbow said to me so many years ago: "You don't want to become known as the town abortionist."

CHAPTER 12

Touch Tobago

Noreen

Being a believer and a doctor, and having a heart for serving others, it was inevitable that at some point I would be attracted to medical missions. My first medical missions trip was to China, through CMDA, the Christian Medical and Dental Association. Our team was there for two weeks, doing mostly surgeries. Haywood stayed home to care for our daughters and our practice. That trip may have been the first, but it was definitely not the only—I did many such trips, in Asia and Africa and elsewhere, always through some organization such as CMDA that sponsored and organized the trip.

One year, after I'd taken a medical missions trip, Haywood and I traveled to my home in Trinidad. One morning, we were talking with Momma in the living room of the home I'd grown up in. I was sharing my experience about the amazing work God does on medical missions trips and she said to me, "You know, you go all over the world helping people. But your people right here in Trinidad could use your help. Why don't you come home and help your own people?"

Her words were like a dagger to my heart. And those words were prophetic. It was as if she spoke that medical mission into being. Soon after, in 2002, Haywood and I launched Touch Tobago with the help of Stuart Quartemont, MD, another medical missionary, one I had gone to Nigeria with. I said, "Stuart, the Lord spoke to me about starting a mission outreach in Tobago. But I have no idea how to start. Would you help me?" He came down with me to Tobago on several occasions and helped me get that medical mission going.

I don't mean to imply that it was easy, or quick, to get all of the pieces to fall into place for something as complicated as that. And it took more knowledge and expertise than Stuart and Haywood and I possessed. One absolutely essential member of the team was my brother Royce, the doctor who practiced in Austin. Besides being brilliant, Royce is always extremely well connected, wherever he goes. He understands not only medicine, but also human behavior and politics. When we sat down with him and explained what we wanted to do with a medical mission to Trinidad and Tobago, he thought for a while and then said, "Well, you'll need to connect with the chief secretary of the Tobago House of Assembly, Orville London." That would be equivalent to a prime minister. Trinidad and Tobago are one republic, but Tobago enjoys relative autonomy.

"How would we meet him?" I said.

"I can connect you with him," Royce said. And he did. In fact, Royce came with Stuart and Haywood and me to Scarborough, Tobago, and introduced us to Mr. Orville London.

As we sat in Mr. London's office—a distinguished-looking Black man with a patch of white in his otherwise black hair, just above his forehead—and explained what we wanted to do, he would listen with interest, nod, and say, "Well, you'll need to talk to So-and-so in the Tobago Health Authority." And he would pick up the phone and let that individual know that we would be calling. "And I want you to see them today," he would say. Click. He'd hang up.

We experienced exceptional favor, and to top it off, Stuart, at the end of our meeting, asked if he could pray for Mr. London. So Stuart laid hands on him and we prayed.

And as we listed, one after the other, our needs and requests, he would contact all the right people on our behalf. And as we would follow up with the people in those offices, they would say, "Oh, yes, Mr. London called about that ..."

As I say, it wasn't easy and it wasn't simple. Haywood and I both needed licenses to practice medicine in Trinidad and Tobago. Since I would be doing surgery, I would need hospital privileges. We would need the proper permits and paperwork to bring huge quantities of medical supplies—including medicine—into Tobago. And as complicated as it all was, that contact, set up by my brother Royce, with one powerful man in Tobago, Orville London, the chief secretary, greased the way for everything that followed. The Tobago Health Authority, the Tobago House of Assembly—

we had introductory letters to all of them, with Mr. Orville London's signature.

If it sounds as if I'm praising Royce and Orville London for making this all work, remember that, while I greatly appreciate and value their contribution, we know it was God who opened the doors for us. So many things came together as a result of "coincidences" we couldn't have foreseen. When I started working to get approved for hospital privileges in Scarborough, for instance, I discovered that one of the hospital's lead doctors was a woman I'd gone to medical school with at Howard in Washington, DC. She walked me through the process, and soon I was approved for surgery in their hospital.

We served both Trinidad and Tobago for almost twenty years. Although we served both islands, we focused our mission on Tobago, because it was more underserved than Trinidad, with fewer resources. On Tobago, the need was greater.

After we launched Touch Tobago, we would go twice a year, for two weeks at a time, taking along medical students, residents of Trinidad or Tobago, people from the church—anybody interested in serving. Our teams included as many as twenty-two people.

Tobago is a relatively small island, only about 120 square miles, located about twenty-two miles northeast of Trinidad and about a hundred miles off the northeast coast of Venezuela. Even if you've never before heard of Tobago, you've been exposed to it. It was one of the sites that influenced the setting of Daniel Defoe's novel *Robinson Crusoe*, and in fact there is a cave on the island called Crusoe Cave. It's also where the 1958 Disney movie *Swiss Family Robinson* was filmed. Compared to much of the rest of the Caribbean, Trinidad and Tobago are wealthy, but that wealth, connected to petroleum production, is concentrated more on Trinidad than Tobago, and medical services on Tobago were widely scattered and difficult to access for some residents, especially those in smaller, more remote villages.

In addition to the way the government opened the door for us, the people loved Touch Tobago too. That was crucial, because if the people don't like and accept you, you'll fail. But we found favor. Our services were without charge, but our patients would bring fruit and other food to show their appreciation.

Touch Tobago was four or five years old when a land-owner leased us a plot of land in a little village (I think the lease was $99 per year). A Methodist church in Houston donated a forty-foot container, fully equipped with a complete HVAC system, electricity, and plumbing that they equipped as a portable medical clinic. Medical Bridges out of Houston donated a wide array of medical supplies to us. What an extravagant gift! We figure it was worth at least $100,000.

The container, loaded with supplies, was shipped to Trinidad on a container ship, then transferred to a barge and transported to Tobago. It was all unloaded in the small village of Charlotteville. The arrival of that forty-foot container, and then moving it down those small streets, was one of the biggest things that had ever happened in that small village. For us, it meant no more having to establish a new site, then setting up and breaking down every day! All of that work, all of that driving back and forth—it had been so challenging for all of us. Having one fixed site meant that people would have to travel further to come to us—but it also meant that we would be able to spend more of each day actually dispensing medical treatment rather than driving, setting up, and tearing down.

Haywood and I had different roles in the mission. I would stay in Charlotteville. I would perform uncomplicated surgical procedures that could be performed under local anesthesia.

I was performing mostly infertility work—not only because, as a gynecologist, I had some familiarity with it, but also because on the islands there are so many women who have either had abortions or have such bad fibroid tumors or endometriosis that it is almost impossible for them to conceive without medical intervention. And in the island culture, if as a woman you can't give a man a baby, then you're no good. You have no value.

My major surgeries were intended to improve women's outcomes with infertility. I was the first one to perform gynecologic laparoscopic surgery on the islands of Trinidad and Tobago.

In the years since 2002, we've seen babies born out of my little efforts to help those women get pregnant. We have some beautiful pictures of babies born to women after I operated on them to help them get pregnant.

Haywood

We had many remarkable experiences there, conducting medical missions on Tobago. One year, before we had the self-contained clinic in the forty-foot container, we rented a diesel van. Not a good idea on an island where, even though it's a petroleum-based economy, there may be only two or three diesel stations.

One morning when we got ready to set out visiting remote locations, we knew that we had to fill the van's tank first thing, because we hadn't been able to get diesel the evening before. We had a long day's drive ahead of us if we were to visit all the locations where we planned to see patients. "Haywood," one of that year's team members said after we'd been driving a while, "Isn't it about time we refill the tank? It's about empty! Where can we get some diesel?"

"That's the big question," I said. "Have you seen any service stations that sell diesel, because I haven't, and I've been looking."

We were driving down the main road as we had that conversation, and a fire station came into view ahead. Beside the fire station was a big above-ground tank with big letters on it: DIESEL.

One of the men in our group said the obvious: "There's diesel right there!"

"Okay," I said.

Desperate, with the needle on the gauge nearing empty, we pulled in and parked in front of the fire department. One of the firemen wandered out and approached us with a curious expression. "Hi," I said. "We're Americans here as part of a medical mission providing free medical care. We're on our way to Castara, and this van runs only on diesel. We're running on fumes now, so we'll never make it to Castara unless we can obtain fuel."

We all climbed out to stretch our legs while the fireman went back inside, presumably to talk to his superior. And sure enough, when he came back out he hopped behind the wheel of the van, backed us up to their big tank, and gave us plenty of diesel to get us to Castara and back. And we spent the rest of the day dispensing vital medical care to people who either couldn't afford it or else had no access to it because of distance or lack of transportation or both.

Even though we were providing medical care and services, we were still representatives of our Lord Jesus Christ, just like any other missionary. We were reminded of that on one occasion in Tobago. We were told about a young local girl with Down's syndrome, about thirteen years old, who wanted to be baptized—but her pastor had denied her request, because he felt it was wrong to baptize someone who was (in his view) incapable of understanding the basic tenets of Christianity: the Trinity, the cross, resurrection. Noreen and I felt that that was so unfortunate, a painful reminder that we believers sometimes cause so much suffering by adhering to the letter of the law but ignoring the spirit. We asked ourselves: *Would Jesus do that? He made it very clear how He felt about children.*

We had with us on that Touch Tobago trip a pastor—not just a pastor, in fact, but a leader in the United Methodist Church. So we held a little church service on the beach and baptized that little girl. And she was so happy! We gave her a little gold cross and chain.

As she was being baptized, a young man walked by, then stopped and watched. "Who are you guys," he asked as soon as she'd been baptized, "and what are you doing?" We told him. Out of nowhere, he said, "I want to be baptized too." It was as if this was an opportunity long wished for.

He was, I believe, a sailor with either the Merchant Marine or the Coast Guard, currently in port in Charlotteville. There was no one preaching at the moment; he wasn't responding to some kind of altar call. The Lord just brought him there, I believe, for that purpose. He was alone, I think—he didn't have any of his crew members with him. But there he was, in our midst, wanting to be baptized. You certainly can't turn away someone like that. He was just wearing street clothes, no uniform, and he took off his shirt—it was, of course, a warm day, given where we were. Our minister baptized him. We handed him a towel, and he dried himself off. And when it was over, he thanked us and went on his way. We never saw him again.

We never know, as we go along trying to fulfill the great commission, who the Lord will put in our path at any given time. That's why we're encouraged in the Word to be ready in season and out of season. I don't know what that man's faith was. I didn't think it was my role to say, "Well, let's see—what church do you go to? Have you been through confirmation? Do you know what baptism is? Have you taken communion?" It's not our role to deny an individual who wants to be baptized. Do you imagine that John the Baptist, as he held a baptismal service, had a page-long questionnaire people had to fill out, and he would refuse to baptize them if they didn't fill it out the right way? Instead, we tried to be sensitive to the Holy Spirit. *This man was led here today for a purpose. And we're here for a purpose.* I don't think God performs counterfeit baptisms. And we aren't representing anyone but the Lord—no denomination, no institution.

When we were in the Caribbean for Touch Tobago, things like that would happen often enough to reassure us that we were in the right place, doing the right things.

Don't you wonder what his faith story was? Had he had an encounter with the Lord while out on ship, out to sea? Had the Spirit urged him, "Be baptized"? And a short time later, he's just walking along the beach and sees a group of people ...

Another beautiful thing about that story is the young girl with Down's syndrome. We all know that many families and many doctors use abortion to "weed out" babies with such conditions as Down's syndrome. In fact, some estimates are that as high as 90 percent of preborn children that test positive for Down's are aborted. I've heard doctors from another country brag that they've all but eradicated Down's in their country. But let's be clear—eradicating Down's is not the same thing as eradicating polio or smallpox. You eradicate smallpox by eradicating a virus. Eradicating Down's means intentionally ending the life of a preborn baby that has the extra chromosome that causes Down's—ending a life. A very different thing. But on that particular day, that beautiful little girl was able to respond to God's invitation to be baptized because someone, rather than choosing abortion, had given her the gift of life. We were grateful to witness it.

Late one day a European family visiting Tobago—Swiss or Swedish, I believe, obviously not from the village—rushed in nearly in a panic. They had been out snorkeling and one of them was attacked by a moray eel. The injured diver was a teenager. The moray eel had grabbed the boy's leg with its razor-sharp teeth and inflicted a multitude of lacerations. We spent approximately two hours with both of us suturing all of his wounds. Thankfully, no arteries, veins, or nerves were severed.

And what teenaged boy wouldn't like having a few scars to show off to his friends while he tells the story of being attacked by a moray eel in Tobago?

They offered to pay, but we explained that we were a medical mission. They did, however, give us a donation.

Some of our Touch Tobago trips turned out to be multi-racial, multi-national trips.

Noreen and I had working with us in our physician's offices a Muslim physician. Her sister was a nurse, and her daughter was a medical assistant—they both worked with us as well. And they came with us, two of them at least, on a Touch Tobago trip. I thought they were quite courageous to come with us, wearing their hijabs since they were still Muslim, hailing from India. People from India are not unheard of in Trinidad and Tobago, but still, for Muslims to go on a Christian outreach was eye opening for me and for them.

Every evening, when we as a team would have our devotions together, our Muslim team members would participate with us, even though they were not Christians. They would talk about what it was like to be in an American grocery store, wearing their hijab, and how it felt when people would look at them and do a double-take with hate-filled eyes. Our Muslim friends were so pained by this that they wept. We told them, "We know we don't have the same belief system as you, but you're our sisters anyway. We're all working together to serve this underserved population. And we love you."

Would I have taken the same attitude toward them when I was a younger believer? Sadly, I suspect not. More likely, I'd have said, "Are you kidding? Have a Muslim, an active, Koran-believing Muslim who doesn't believe in the Christian faith, doesn't believe in Jesus as her personal savior, participating in a Christian mission? Participating as a doctor, no less? Isn't that just inviting the devil in? What's she going to say when some deathly ill person asks her to pray with them?"

Now, I would take the view that Jesus ministers to everyone, including doctors. And Muslim doctors who participate in Christian missions. Who's to say how the lives of those Muslim women might have been changed by what they saw, heard, and did with Touch Tobago?

CHAPTER 13

The Great Escape

Haywood

Of course, Noreen and I have not been the only people active in the abortion industry who, convicted by God about their participation in it and about the lives lost, turned their backs on it. We are not the only ones who, then, became active in the pro-life movement. There have been many others. And, God willing, there will be many more.

One of the best known is Abby Johnson. Some readers are undoubtedly already familiar with Abby's story through her book *Unplanned* or through the feature film of the same title based on the book. I won't repeat the whole story here, since it's so widely known, but in this sixty-second version, Abby was the director of a Planned Parenthood facility in Bryan, Texas, near where Noreen and I lived and practiced. One day Abby was called into the procedure room to assist in an ultrasound-guided abortion. As she moved the ultrasound transducer across the patient's belly, Abby saw on the monitor, for the first time, what actually happens during an abortion.

From *Unplanned* (Abby Johnson with Cindy Lambert, Chicago, Tyndale House Publishers, 2014, pp. 5, 6, 7):

I had a sudden urge to yell, "Stop!" To shake the woman and to say, "Look what is happening to your baby! Wake up! Hurry! Stop them!"

But even as I thought those words, I looked at my own hand holding the probe. I was one of "them" performing this act. My eyes shot back to the screen again. The cannula was already being rotated by the doctor, and now I could see the tiny body violently twisting with it. For the briefest moment it looked as if the baby were being wrung like a dishcloth, twirled and squeezed. And then the little body crumpled and began disappearing into the cannula before my eyes. The last thing I saw was the tiny, perfectly formed backbone sucked into the tube, and then everything was gone. And the uterus was empty. Totally empty ...

My eyes traveled back to my own hands. I looked at them as if they weren't even my own.

How much damage have these hands done over the past eight years? How many lives have been taken because of them? Not just because of my hands, but because of my words. What if I'd known the truth, and what if I'd told all those women?

Shaken to her core, Abby knew that she could never again participate in an abortion. Nor, she decided, could she continue to promote them. She would have to leave Planned Parenthood.

Even though many of the staff and volunteers of BVCL (later renamed 40 Days for Life) had spoken to Abby along the fence that separated the sidewalk, where we prayed, from the Planned Parenthood facility, Noreen and I didn't know her personally. But we knew who she was. One day, I stepped into the hospital doctor's lounge, and my phone rang. I glanced at the screen—Shawn, executive director of BVCL. It had been a trying day and I needed some rest, but I'd learned that I need to take Shawn's calls.

"Haywood!" he said, so excited he could barely contain himself. "Haywood, you won't believe what just happened. Abby Johnson just came to our office. She's leaving Planned Parenthood."

What? How could Abby Johnson be leaving Planned Parenthood? She was the local director!

Shawn went on to tell me how earlier that day Abby had come into his office, weeping, and had related to him her experience with the ultrasound-assisted abortion and her conviction that she could no longer serve an organization that performed or promoted abortions, now that she'd seen with her own eyes what abortions really do to those tiny human beings.

Abby knew that Noreen and I were active with BVCL and that we were physicians who frequently spoke out against abortion. So the next day after her surprise visit to the BVCL offices, Abby came to our office and sat down with us to tell us what had happened. The experience was still raw for her, and although she wasn't weeping, she was trembling, clearly frightened, and she told us her story in a shaking voice. We listened, recognizing that, for Abby, this was a similar kind of life-changing revelation Noreen and I had experienced that day at the altar at Aldersgate Church. I didn't have any window into Abby's emotions, so I certainly can't claim to know what she was feeling, but given her circumstances, I would guess that she was feeling the same combination of relief, freedom, and foreboding that you might feel when you escape from a Stockholm syndrome situation, or when, having been a victim of human trafficking, you are finally freed from the control of the trafficker who has harmed you. Yes, now you're free. Now you can envision a fresh new life. But are they coming after you? Will they try as an act of vengeance to harm or perhaps even kill you or someone close to you?

Shawn had the same concern:

All of us in the Coalition were ecstatic. The joy I felt at seeing Abby, someone I'd known for eight years, have a change of heart cannot be put into words. But I felt a check deep in my soul. The Irish are gifted at finding the worst in every situation, and despite my joy, I knew that not everyone would be joyful. Abby would need protection. I was waiting for the other shoe to drop. Planned Parenthood directors do not have conversions and resign from their jobs. And they certainly do not join "the other side" and start praying outside their own clinics! It had never happened before. Planned Parenthood, I suspected, would want to make sure it never happened again. (David Bereit and Shawn Carney with Cindy Lambert, *40 Days for Life: Discover What God Has Done … Imagine What He Can Do, Expanded Edition,* Nashville, Tennessee: Cappella Books, 2017, page 116)

Their fears, Abby's and Shawn's, were well founded—a few weeks later, Planned Parenthood filed lawsuits against both of them, seeking an injunction intended to silence them. The irony is that neither of them had gone public. It was publicity resulting from the lawsuit that caused talk show hosts across the country to approach this privacy-seeking former Planned Parenthood director as their guest, and that resulted eventually in a bestselling book and a feature film.

I think we can safely say Planned Parenthood's game plan backfired.

Oh—and that visit Abby made to our office after she left Planned Parenthood? We tried to reassure her: "Everything's going to be okay. It's going to work out."

But as it turns out, she hadn't come seeking reassurance. She had come to ask us, "Do you have any openings for a receptionist or other positions?" Not for herself. She was asking because she thought a couple of her former co-workers at Planned Parenthood might be ripe to leave the abortion industry, and if so she wanted to make it easier for them by providing them with a landing spot. Unfortunately, we didn't have any openings in our office. But I'm happy to see that that generosity of spirit is still true of Abby—her ministry, And Then There Were None, exists to find those many who have been unhappy or convicted in the abortion industry and encourage and ease their transition to life outside that industry.

It's a funny thing. Planned Parenthood always says, "Abortion is only a small part of our services." But if that's the case, why are so many abortion facilities closing down in states where they can no longer do abortions? One of the things Abby told us after she left Planned Parenthood was she had been, as the facility director, encouraged to do more abortions, because Planned Parenthood made most of its money through abortion.

One day Shawn got another piece of useful information from Abby. Here's how he relates it in *40 Days for Life* (Expanded Edition, Nashville, Tennessee, Cappella Books, 2017, p. 265-66):

"Shawn, Bryan is closing!" Abby's voice, vibrating with excitement, bounced out of the phone.

"What? What are you talking about?" I felt as if a jolt of electricity had just shot through me. Had she said what I thought she'd said?

"My clinic—the Bryan clinic—Planned Parenthood is shutting it down!"

I was afraid to believe what sounded too good to be true. I needed facts.

"Are you sure? How do you know? What happened?" I blurted, not even pausing to breathe between questions.

Abby told me she'd just received a Planned Parenthood news release on her phone reporting they were closing three of their Texas centers—ours in College Station/Bryan and two others. "I'm forwarding it to you right now," she said.

By this time I had pulled up a media article online reporting the same thing.

Every ounce of me wanted to rejoice with her, but I needed to get confirmation from the horse's mouth.

"Abby, this is too good to be true. I need some confirmation," I said. "I'm calling Planned Parenthood headquarters myself. I'll call you right back."

[...]

"It's true! It's really true!" I shouted, laughing, jumping up from my chair and bouncing around my office. "I always knew it would one day close its doors, but I didn't expect it now, so soon, so suddenly! Can you believe this!" I wanted to shout it from the rooftop!

[...]

I don't want you to miss the irony here: I was now describing the closure of the facility at 4112 East 29th Street as "so soon" and "so sudden." I'm certain that, until that moment, our waiting through fifteen years of untold hours of prayer by many thousands of people had never before seemed soon or sudden. It had seemed long—very, very long. In fact, it had often appeared endless, especially during thunderstorms, blistering heat, a few flying eggs from passing cars, and the constant sight of a busy abortion facility with no signs of closure in sight. Campaign after campaign, abortion after abortion, week after week, year after year. But God's timing, as usual, was perfect.

What were Noreen and I thinking and feeling when we heard the news? And when, a short time later, we participated in the celebration 40 Days for Life threw to celebrate the closing?

Early in that celebration, a local pastor spoke and confessed that he hadn't believed that the Bryan office of Planned Parenthood was going to close. If I'd felt that way, I don't think I'd have had the motivation to come out for our 40 Days for Life prayer vigils in the dark and cold of night, in thunderstorms, in the face of shouted insults from passing cars. I wouldn't have found the strength to keep up a busy speaking schedule requiring long hours, lots of preparation, and many days away from home. To commit to those things, I have to believe that the Bible is true. That the fervent prayers of the righteous are effective. That when we pray God listens.

I would love to have seen it happen sooner—as Shawn said, fifteen years is a long time. A lot of abortions. But the timing of answered prayer is in God's hands. We can't force it. Still, I have to believe that God loves these little babies far more than I could, just as He loves me far more than I could ever imagine. So if that facility is killing the babies He lovingly formed while still inside their mothers, then I have to believe He wants that place to close more than I do.

I understand the amazement behind the words when I hear someone say, "I just never thought the place would close!" I've heard it often. Life is filled with trials and tribulations, and when something goes right, we're often amazed, even if we prayed for it. But *of course it was going to close! God is faithful. That's how He proves who He is.* We've seen that, over and over again, in the Bible, especially in the Old Testament. He wants to show how He works through his people. We are His prize creation. He knits together every one of us within our mother's womb. He created us in His image. He hates abortion. So of course, in His own timing, He will reach out His hand against it.

And think what God accomplished in those fifteen years, because that Planned Parenthood facility was there! What man intended for evil, God used for good. He used the presence of Planned Parenthood to motivate and empower those of us who were there to launch first the BVCL and then 40 Days for Life, which now has a global impact.

And if you look back at that first meeting at St. Mary's Catholic Church, when the coming of Planned Parenthood to Bryan/College Station had just been announced, we had no idea what to do. We were like the Jews when they first left Egypt, feeling as if they were just wandering around in the desert. But that day all God was saying to us was, *All I need is your obedience and faithfulness.* Who was there at that first meeting? People who were willing to take a stand but needed leadership. Students at Texas A&M who were willing to volunteer for whatever we needed them to do. To be fair, I have to admit that most of the men active in the movement in our town were pulled into it by women, primarily Catholic women. David Bereit, Shawn, and I—we all followed the lead of Lauren Gulde and many other women who picked up the torch first.

And isn't that a model of how discipleship works? We hear the message, we see it in people's lives, and then we go get somebody else, just like Andrew did after he met Jesus. "Come see the man!" Or the woman at the well, "Come hear the man who told me everything I ever did!"

Noreen and I feel so blessed to have been witnesses to this demonstration of God's power. What a privilege! How many people get to see such overt evidence of God's power? How many communities? One day it's open, the next day it's closed. So yeah, we got excited about that!

When we heard that they were actually closing the facility, of course we wondered: Is Planned Parenthood actually willing to admit defeat in this community by closing the doors? They were definitely closing them—but would they reopen, here or elsewhere nearby? We knew that much of the impetus for the closing was financial. It takes a lot of money to keep an operation like that going, and any organization, no matter how well funded, can lose only a limited amount of money on any one facility over time.

Noreen

When, in 2013, the announcement was made that the Planned Parenthood facility was closing and that the building was listed for sale, Haywood and I were still volunteering at Hope Pregnancy Center. We were both asked to be keynote speakers at their annual fundraiser. The Lord had already given Hope a dream and desire to purchase the former Planned Parenthood building as an expansion of its ministry into STD screening, treatment, and abstinence counseling. So when we spoke, the Lord prompted me to pray like Jabez—a bold prayer that He expand our territory, in faith that He would bless us indeed. My presentation that night was called, "What If?" What if the Lord would transform that building from a place that took lives, to a place that rescued lives? The Lord humbled me that night in front of that large audience by leading me to declare my sorrow over all the babies whose lives I had taken by abortion. And further, He prompted me to ask the audience's forgiveness for what I had done to the women, men, and families who had suffered the consequences of the abortions I'd performed. "I can never repay you for the harm I inflicted on your lives," I said, "but I can pray for God to heal your pain and suffering. Standing here tonight, I renew my pledge to all of you that I am committed to doing all I can to stop abortion—whether by action, by committing whatever resources Haywood and I have, or by the word of my testimony." When I finished, there was hardly a dry eye in the house.

A year later Hope teamed up with 40 Days for Life to purchase the newly closed Planned Parenthood building on East 29th Street. Haywood and I were invited to move our medical office into that very building. Imagine, two former abortionists, now working in pro-life ministry and practicing medicine, all in a former, now-closed Planned Parenthood facility—the same Planned Parenthood building, in fact, that those two former abortionists had often stood in front of, on the same sidewalk with housewives, pastors, college students, and others praying that God would save the babies in the wombs of the women walking into that building.

And just as we prayed—so had it happened. And more besides.

Just look at God!

CHAPTER 14

We Fight Forward

Haywood

Some years ago, I was invited to speak at a pro-life fundraising banquet in Grand Rapids, Michigan. The city is known for its generosity to certain causes, including the cause of life, so it's a popular place for nonprofits or political groups to come to do their fundraising, even from far outside Michigan. The banquet was held in a big, luxurious room at the Marriott, and it was filled with people in beautiful, expensive clothes—guys who, unlike at most pro-life fundraising efforts, were actually wearing tuxedos. Clearly, there was wealth in this crowd.

In this case, it wasn't some out-of-state group doing their fundraising, but rather a local Grand Rapids pro-life group. That group was led by Jim Sprague, CEO of PRC Grand Rapids. It was Jim who had invited me up to speak at their event. Earlier that day, when we still had some time before the banquet, he had asked whether I wanted to see the infamous 72 Ransom Avenue. I knew well the story of that building, by word of mouth but also by the account my good friend David Bereit had written in *40 Days for Life: Discover What God Has Done ... Imagine What He Can Do, Expanded Edition* (Cappella Books, 2017). The building itself had a long and mostly distinguished history. It had been built in the late nineteenth century as a Jewish synagogue, Congregation Emanuel. In 1949, when the Jewish congregation was ready to move to a larger facility, they sold the building to Holy Trinity Greek Orthodox Church. Eventually, Holy Trinity, too, outgrew the building, and sold it to an investor's group whose intention was to turn a profit. They were able to get the zoning changed to commercial, after which they leased 72 Ransom Avenue to the highest bidder: Heritage Clinic for Women, which became the largest abortion facility in western Michigan. After a hundred years as a sanctuary for worshipping God, 72 Ransom Avenue became the site where over twenty thousand preborn children would be aborted over a period of eight years.

Not surprisingly, many local Christians were appalled that a former place of worship had been turned to such a nefarious purpose, and a group of their leaders began meeting regularly to pray that they would be able to reclaim that building for God.

Four years later, when the new owners put the building up for sale, many of those leaders wondered, *Is this the answer to our prayers?* And they tried diligently to find the financing to purchase it, but for four years, one obstacle after another arose. During those years, they launched a ministry called LIFE International whose goal was to establish pregnancy resource centers in every nation around the world where abortions are performed. One of their first goals: to purchase 72 Ransom Avenue and turn it into the headquarters of LIFE International.

Finally—in late 2003, that group of praying leaders was able to put together a deal that the owners of 72 Ransom Avenue were willing to accept. In early 2004, the new owners kicked the abortionist out. LIFE International moved in and began setting the property up as their new HQ.

So when Jim led me into the building on Ransom Avenue, at first it was much like touring any other modern ministry headquarters—offices filled with smiling people, modern equipment, and plaques and photographs on the wall that pointed to some of their proudest moments. But there was much that wasn't at all like touring a typical office suite—such as the stories some of the staff told me about, when they first moved in, walking slowly from room to room praying that any evil spirits still present from the building's days as an abortion facility would be removed.

And there was more, just as there had been when my friend David had toured the building a few years before.

At the end of my tour, Jim led me down to the procedures room where the abortions had actually been performed. That room had been left just as it had been when the infamous abortion doctor had been using it. It hadn't been cleaned—and it was far from sanitary. The Mayo stand was still next to the table, still covered with a towel and stocked with the instruments a doctor would have used to perform an abortion.

This was the first time I'd been in such a room since I was performing abortions myself, back in California, many years before. To say that I was profoundly affected would be an understatement, and knowing Jim, that's why he set up my tour of their offices this way, with the procedures room last.

I recognized each of the instruments on the Mayo stand—the dilators, the curette, the tenaculum, and all the rest. Automatically, I reached out to pick one of them up to examine it—and I couldn't do it. I couldn't touch it. The memories of having used instruments like these to perform abortions myself were simply too visceral, even though it had been many years. I didn't want to feel them against my skin. I pulled my hand back.

The instruments were laid out correctly on the surgical towel, lined up from left to right in the order that the abortionist would have used them. So they had clearly been laid out by someone familiar with the procedure. Had this same Mayo stand been sitting here since the former occupant, the abortionist, had been kicked out?

Speaking of the abortionist—I remembered something David Bereit had said after he'd been in this room, and I looked down at the linoleum floor. It was true. There where the doctor's feet had been positioned for twenty thousand abortions, he had worn a definite depression in the linoleum from the pressure of his feet.

Twenty thousand times!

The man was gone, but the impact of his choices remained—not just in the linoleum I stood on, but in the families deprived of the presence and influence of the unique human beings whose lives the abortionist had ended. God had a purpose for those tiny lives when He formed them *in the womb*. What that purpose was, we will never know. God sent those little ones to us—and one abortionist sent twenty thousand of them straight back to God.

I was vaguely aware that Jim was watching me. "I wonder if this thing still works," he said, sliding his hand along the side of the suction pump used in abortions. "I don't even know if it's still plugged in." He hit the switch.

The pump started. That familiar sound that accompanies the sucking out of the contents of the womb—the dismemberment and maceration of a small human being. It threw me back into the experience of being in a room much like this one in the days when I was the abortionist. Suddenly I was crushed. My lower extremities weakened. I just about lost it. As I hastily left the room, Jim turned it off. "Yep, still hooked up." He looked up. "Now, let me show you our prayer room." As we moved next door, he looked at me a little more carefully and said quietly, "Are you okay?"

No, I wasn't okay. My own emotions were raw, now that I saw abortion for what it was and had been forced back into reliving the experience of being the man with the suction curette in his hand. But perhaps even worse was the realization that, when I was performing abortions, my emotions had been the same as any other doctor who does them—which is to say, almost nothing. It was mechanical, cold. I had been thoroughly desensitized. And sure, I could blame the medical community that had normalized the violent death of the preborn, but in truth, there was no one to blame but myself. I'd made choices. I had allowed this.

I had allowed myself to become desensitized to the point

that, during a day of abortions, I just wanted to get as many done as possible as fast as possible—and collect my money for doing it. *Yeah, let me finish this one up, and then—you got the next one set up? I need to finish the rest quick so I can get my butt out of here. Stuff to do. Got my check ready?*

But the women, confused and grieved, who left the facility after I had performed their abortions didn't have quite so cavalier an attitude, I'm sure.

A few hours later, I stepped up to the podium at the fundraising banquet. But I made a few changes in the talk I'd planned to give that night. I wanted to try to recapture for the audience the emotions, the realizations, I'd had that very afternoon at 72 Ransom Avenue. "Let me tell you about something that happened to me just today," I said, seeing Jim out in the audience, nodding.

Judging from the audience's response, it was one of the most effective parts of my talk that night. It was fresh. It had the feel of something just experienced. I'm sure that many of the people there that night had read *40 Days for Life*, which included David Bereit's account of his visit there, but no one had yet heard it related by someone who had himself performed abortions—and had to live with the memory.

To me, one of the most profound and exciting parts of the story of the pro-life movement taking over that building was something that neither David nor I actually saw, but that rather was related to us by those who, through their years of effort and prayer, helped to make that takeover happen and experienced it firsthand. As David related it in *40 Days for Life* (Expanded Edition, Nashville, Tennessee, Cappella

Books, 2017, p. 98), the next Sunday night, after the building had been purchased and the abortionist kicked out:

> A group of nine LIFE International board members gathered in the entryway to pray over this former church that had become an abortion center—to reclaim it for God.
>
> Someone suggested, "Why don't we start our prayers wherever the abortionist would start his day every morning?" So they went downstairs, past all the rooms, all the way to the back hall, where a large metal door opened out into the alley where the abortionist would park his car. They decided to start their prayers in that hall near the large, closed door.
>
> They gathered in a circle. They held hands. And they prayed fervently for God to reclaim this building. When they were finished, the new director for LIFE International, Kurt Dillinger, closed their prayer by saying "Amen."
>
> At that moment, the empty building's silence was shattered as the big steel door—which had been closed and latched—burst open, swinging wildly outward to slam against the bricks of the building's alley wall. All who stood there felt a rush of air go out the door. A few seconds later, they felt a gentle breeze come back in. They were stunned. A board member asked, "What just happened?" Shaken, another board member pulled the door closed and said, "I think something just left in a hurry."

I think that board member had it right. I think something left in a hurry. When Satan and his forces come up against the power of the Holy Spirit, Satan will not prevail.

And just as, we believe, some evil spirit vacated that building that day in the face of the effectual prayer of faithful followers of Christ, I think the story of my life and Noreen's is the story of two people living for themselves and seeking their own worldly definition of success to the extent that they were willing to sacrifice innocents to achieve it. But God will not be denied, and He sought us out, kicked out the "old man," and installed a new man (and woman!) in his place. I have never regretted it.

Since God turned my life around that day at Aldersgate Church in College Station, Texas, I have tried to live a life worthy of Christ's sacrifice on my behalf. Given our time, early in our careers, as active abortion doctors, part of what "a life worthy" means to us is engaging daily in the fight against abortion. I will stick with that fight. And I hope that, after reading this book, you will too.

I'm old enough that I lived as an adult through the entire half-century of Roe v. Wade's attack on the preborn—nearly all of that time as a doctor. Some of my memories of the very beginning of that Supreme Court decision are still vivid. For instance, I clearly remember seeing, in 1973, a political cartoon by the famous cartoonist Karl Hubenthal, published in the *Los Angeles Herald Examiner* (which ceased publication in 1989). The cartoon showed a stooped, elderly person staring at a wall that bore a graffiti message: "Roe v. Wade." The caption for the cartoon? "Handwriting on the wall."

I was a junior in college at the time, and at first, the connection escaped me. Maybe my youth was blinding me. It didn't take long before I saw the connection clearly: If Roe v. Wade stands, then the elderly may be the next group of humans to be in danger of being deemed disposable. If we can establish laws that protect our "right" to put the preborn to death, then why not those too old and frail to contribute fully to society, those who are simply "taking up valuable resources"?

But now, fifty years later, the tables have been turned, as we all know. Roe v. Wade was overturned by the Supreme Court on June 24, 2022. Much has been written and spoken about that momentous decision, and I'm not going to attempt now to write a lengthy treatise on it. But some things, I believe, do need to be said.

First, many of you will remember that, before the decision that became known as Dobbs v. Jackson Women's Health Organization overturning Roe v. Wade was announced or even finalized, something unprecedented happened: There was a leak of Justice Alito's draft opinion in that case that, while not final, suggested which direction the decision might go. No "leaker" was ever identified. It served as a good reminder to us all that even the highest court in the land is compromised and its integrity permanently marred. To the present time, no one has been held accountable. To leak something like that? Amazing, and a definite first for the US Supreme Court to my knowledge.

Second, I find it very reassuring that the Supreme Court

corrected an earlier decision—even one from fifty years ago—that was greatly flawed in the first place. Made up out of thin air, I've often said. I believe that most legal scholars recognized Roe v. Wade as a flawed decision that would eventually be overturned. Certainly the former Supreme Court justice Ruth Bader Ginsburg, as liberal as she was, was no fan of the logical and legal underpinning of the Roe decision and thought it was the wrong decision to resolve the abortion question. So I think it can be said that any questions about the integrity of the Supreme Court that might have been raised by the leak of Justice Alito's draft opinion were answered—and the court's standing redeemed—by a powerful and right-minded decision in Dobbs.

Third—Yes, definitely we should celebrate the Dobbs decision. It reassures us about the effectiveness and wisdom of the highest court of the land. Are the Supreme Court justices human beings? Can they make mistakes? Of course, just as any political or legal entity from any political party can. But they did indeed later think better of it, in this case, and correct their error—in the same way previous courts corrected the Dred Scott decision (which held that the US Constitution did not extend American citizenship to people of Black African descent, and thus they could not enjoy the rights and privileges the Constitution conferred upon American citizens) and the Plessy v. Ferguson decision (which held that state-mandated segregation laws did not violate the equal protection clause of the Fourteenth Amendment).

As thankful as we should be that those two earlier decisions were overturned, remember this: There weren't sixty million people who lost their lives because of the Dred Scott Decision. There weren't sixty million people who lost their lives because of Plessy v. Ferguson. Yes, there were lives lost because of both of those decisions. Yes, there was great injustice as well. But Roe v. Wade led to the slaughter of more than sixty million innocent preborn babies in the US alone. Which was the greater evil? We don't need to resolve that question. Evil is evil. But if those preborn had a voice ...

Fourth—and I'm speaking particularly now to the pro-life movement at large: Yes, we can celebrate this decision that we have prayed for and worked for for so long. Yes, go ahead—jump for joy! But don't make the mistake of thinking that we can now safely spike the football in the end zone, yell "We won! We won!" and call the job over and done. Thousands of babies are still being aborted daily—right here in the US where Roe v. Wade has been overturned.

Changing sports references: As a lifelong Dodgers fan (remember, I grew up in Los Angeles), I remember that electric moment in game one of the 1988 World Series, Dodgers vs. Oakland Athletics. An injured, limping Kirk Gibson— with *two* bad legs—came to bat as a pinch hitter with two outs in the bottom of the ninth inning against feared Athletics closer Dennis Eckersley. Barely able to stand at the plate and swing the bat, and with two strikes, Gibson blasted a homerun to right field that with one stroke won the game for the Dodgers. The Athletics had been heavily favored to take the series, but, inspired by Gibson's heroism, the Dodgers won it in five games. Anyone who watched that game probably still has Vin Scully's line ringing in their ears: "They are going wild at Dodger Stadium! No one wants to leave!"

For pro-lifers, the overturning of Roe v. Wade can function much like that famous homerun by Kirk Gibson, often ranked among the top ten moments in sports. It inspired the Dodgers to play at their best, to not give up. As a result, they won not just the battle but the war. And we too need to continue to battle. The battle against abortion is no more won than the World Series was won in 1988 when Gibson hit that homerun—in game one. They still needed three more victories. So they buckled down and set in to get them.

To be sure, there are many states where abortion laws are now rightly protecting the lives of the preborn. But it's also true that many states are doubling down on ensuring access to abortion and protecting abortion itself, trying to make sure it stays available forever, even adding it to their state constitutions as a right. Many readers of this book live in those very states. We still have a lot of work to do. Take a moment to pray a prayer of thanksgiving for what the overturning of Roe v. Wade has accomplished—and then let's decide what *you* need to do next and get back to work.

Fifth, here's an analogy that might illuminate where we are at this point in our nation's history: Imagine an alternative history for the US in which, before the Emancipation Proclamation, slavery is a fact of life all across the US instead of just in the South. People in every state can buy, sell, and enslave people. And now imagine that the Emancipation Proclamation is signed, freeing the enslaved people—but not *all*, because in this version of our history, it's still legal to own and to buy and sell people in the South. In other words, in this story, the Emancipation Proclamation basically brings us back to the situation found in the country in our *actual* history before the Civil War. That decision would have freed many thousands of enslaved people, and it would have been cause for rejoicing. But it would not have been time to relax and consider the battle won. People would have still been, at least in the South, a huge swath of the country, denied basic freedoms and grossly mistreated. It would have been necessary to continue to press the fight to end slavery—just as we must continue the fight to end abortion.

What we want is not just the overturning of Roe v. Wade. That is now a fact. What we want is what the founders of our nation wrote in the Declaration of Independence:

> We hold these truths to be self-evident, that all men are created equal, that they are endowed by their Creator with certain unalienable Rights, that among these are Life, Liberty and the pursuit of Happiness.

Notice that the Declaration of Independence does not say that we have the right to life, liberty, and the pursuit of happiness because we have been granted those rights by the US government. We have those rights because they were given to us by God—"endowed by their Creator." The government should simply recognize those God-given rights. Just as it was hypocritical of the government to claim that white men had a full slate of rights, such as the right to vote, but that women and nonwhite people did not, it is hypocritical of the government now to say that the rest of us have the right to life but that preborn people do not.

The government must recognize these rights.

And that is what we fight for.

My Noreen

NOT LONG AFTER WE FIRST MET HIM, DR. PHILLIP NEY analyzed the spiritual genetic background of Noreen Johnson, my first wife and mother of my two youngest daughters. "Your spiritual DNA," he told her, "is that of a missionary."

Even before he told her that, she had become active in medical missions, participating in numerous overseas medical mission trips. And she continued her commitment to that call on her life after her mother challenged her to serve those in need in Trinidad and Tobago. "You know, you go all over the world helping people, but your people right here in Trinidad could use your help. Why don't you come home and help your own people?" Noreen responded to this prophetic exhortation by working tirelessly to establish the medical missions outreach we named Touch Tobago, which she and I led for nearly twenty years.

And right to the end: Noreen was preparing for another medical missions trip in the summer of 2021 to Nigeria, but she tested positive for COVID-19.

She was unable to make that final missions trip. She didn't recover from COVID and left us on August 28, 2021.

Noreen was a doctor extraordinaire. She was skilled and committed when I first met her during our years as residents at Martin Luther King Jr./Charles R. Drew Medical Center in Los Angeles, and she diligently developed her skills throughout her career. She not only brought gynecologic laparoscopic surgery to Trinidad and Tobago but also pioneered robotic surgery in our community of Bryan/College Station, Texas. Over the years, I assisted her in surgery countless times. She would remind me, as she delicately handled the tissue, "The tissue must be respected. No chop chop!" If ever an urgent issue arose during a surgery, I marveled as she would handle it so calmly. She attributed much of this to one of her mentors at Howard University College of Medicine, the late Dr. LaSalle Leffall, a globally famous surgeon. He would often state that an essential trait of a successful surgeon is to exhibit *equanimity under duress*, and boy did she do it! She employed this same principle outside the surgical suite, in everyday matters—but using a similar version that our children could understand: *More speed, less haste.*

But Noreen's medical skills weren't her only vehicle for impacting people's lives. She was a formidable woman who was able to influence every area of the lives of those around her—personally, professionally, spiritually. Her children, for instance, reflected her spirit.

Why do so many people who go to church every Sunday

and think of themselves as "active Christians" have little discernible impact on the lives of others while someone like Noreen has so much? Much of it has to do, I believe, with the many words of prophecy spoken over Noreen over the years, as well as her obedience in making her life available to the Lord.

That obedience had its effect. It resulted in a balance in Noreen's life as an exemplary wife, mother, missionary, and medical professional that was notable, to say the least.

Kaishauna, my firstborn, always had an excellent relationship with Udelle and Riva and continues to enjoy leading her younger sisters. Kaishauna and Riva are both physicians. Kaishauna is an internist specializing in Hospice Palliative Medicine. Riva is a Functional Medical Specialist. Udelle, a writer and linguist, is our creative arm.

Noreen and I also "adopted" numerous young ladies over the years, including Virginia when she was a junior at Texas A&M. She went on to attend medical school there and is now a practicing OBGYN.

Noreen's memorial service was a unique presentation: music, video, and tributes. All who attended thought it tailor-made for her. Her family felt it captured her passion, culture, and life's work.

Life without Noreen brought challenges, as did the stark reality of being a widower. Many of you have also experienced this. I cherish the past and embrace the future, knowing "weeping may endure for the night, but joy comes in the morning" (Psalm 30:5 NKJV).

Noreen and I will meet again.

Acknowledgments

Jesus Christ is the Author and Finisher of my faith. I am eternally grateful that He rescued me from darkness and welcomed me into His glorious light. Truly God continues to redeem all things for our good and His glory. Without Him, this work would not have been realized.

A multitude of men and women have discipled me as a believer; others still have mentored me or been co-laborers in the fight for humanity. I love and appreciate you.

And finally, I thank my new bride, Daphne Harris Robinson, LAS, for her significant role and contributions in completing this book. Not only is she my helpmate, but I am blessed to have her as my ministry partner. Together we serve internationally and collaborate in family, life, pregnancy care, abortion recovery, and reconciliation ministry, as well as medical missions. Through our marriage, we have eight living children and thirteen who are with the Lord; a host of "bonus" sons and daughters; five grandchildren; and one great grandchild. Here's to forty-one!

I love you, Mrs. Robinson.

PRAY TO END ABORTION
40 DAYS FOR LIFE.
WWW.40DAYSFORLIFE.COM

40 DAYS FOR LIFE

BE PART OF
The beginning of the end of abortion

PRAY!
Find your closest 40 Days for Life vigil location at www.40daysforlife.com/location

READ!
Keep up with saved lives, abortion worker conversions, and the pulse of the pro-life movement by receiving *Day 41*, the quarterly magazine, for FREE! Sign up at www.40daysforlife.com/magazine

LISTEN!
Download the weekly 40 Days for Life podcast for free. Guests include Peter Kreeft, Mark Houck, Eric Metaxas, Benjamin Watson, Lila Rose, and many more. Listen at any podcast app or www.40daysforlife.com/podcast

WATCH!
The 40 Days for Life Podcast is closing in on ONE MILLION downloads—and it's now available in video format! Watch the weekly podcast and all of our informative and inspirational videos at www.40daysforlife.com/videos

REPRESENT!
Open yourself to being a witness for the unborn while wearing our 40 Days for Life gear. Allow God to work through you to help you courageously speak up for the unborn. For 40 Days for Life apparel, signs, books and media, and promotional materials, visit www.40daysforlifegear.com